The Four Faced Liar

Issue 01
November 2022

@the4facedliar

@the4facedliar

the4facedliar.com

Editors: Patrick Holloway
           Lucy Holme
           Stephen Brophy
           Rosie Morris

Contents

The Four Faced Liar
Issue 01

ISBN No. 978-1-914488-86-3

Cover art: 'Shandon Bells' (2019) by Shane O' Driscoll,
Cover font: Adobe Caslon Pro
Internal font: Baskerville (designed in the 1750s by John Baskerville)

Printed in Ireland by Lettertec on 100gsm paper

www.lettertec.com

Editorial

'Under the Four-Faced Liar it is 3 am…The iron tongue of Shandon Steeple is silent now and the great clocks on its four faces merely click and cluck and grumble quietly as they haggle amongst themselves.'

— The Four-Faced Liar (2020) Ger Fitzgibbon

The inaugural issue of The Four Faced Liar might have its roots firmly bedded in the streets of Cork City but like the melodic toll of the iconic Shandon bells it resounds with stories, reflections, accents, vernacular and perspectives from not only Ireland but from much further afield, signalling its arrival as an international journal of prose, poetry, translation and visual art. We might have to admit to a fair amount of clicking, clucking, haggling and grumbling ourselves during the exhilarating (and new to us) process of putting together a journal and perhaps we began to inhabit the spirit of the great clockface itself as we looked outwards over Cork and beyond to create what we consider to be an incredible and diverse anthology. Issue One features the unflinching work of artists and writers hailing from England, Scotland, The Isle of Man, Germany, Greece, Canada, Nigeria, Bulgaria and the USA to name a few. There are meandering road trips, such as the one taken by plucky Ruth winding through the peat moss glens of Ulster, in Jan Carson's compelling short story 'Grand So', and ruminations on the familiar and unfamiliar landscape encountered while traversing memory such as those of the narrator in emerging writer Malinda Meadow's poem of loss and reflection. Some stories such as Karla Hirsch's dystopian flash 'The Roommate' and Mark Thomas' 'Dreams of Fish' transport us to disorientating and dreamlike worlds but we are returned home to the everyday moments of Irish life with Billy Fenton's 'Bird' and Dean Fee's 'Ireland's First Serial Killer'. There are stark moments of honest contemplation explored in Nidhi Zak/ Aria Eipe's forensic examination of heartbreak and intimacy and in Mary O' Donnell's poetic tributes to the bravery and quiet stoicism of war victims. Alongside more established names we welcome poets such as Yanita Georgieva, Ewan Monaghan, Simon Maddrell and Sodïq Oyèkànmí. We also feature the first of our interview series with Cork novelist Danny Denton who was instrumental in bringing the four editors together. The issue is rounded out with CNF and translation that jumped out at us from the incredible and overwhelming number of submissions we received. Some of the thematic concerns which we happily excavated during our reading period included the vagaries and idiosyncrasies of language, unconventional living arrangements, the indelible traces of ancestry, awkward and unforgettable dinner encounters, lost love, the voiceless and defenceless casualties of war and some beautifully flawed humans just searching for a safe place to make sense of the madness of conflict and the magical mundanity of the ordinary. These are the strands of brilliance which rose to the surface during our first call for submissions in June and we read so many hundreds of pieces which made us think, weep and shout out in recognition, it is amazing to see them all here together in a celebration of so many unique viewpoints. The pages of the magazine are brightened further by six pieces of outstanding visual art from international contributors. Cover art for issue one is Shandon Bells by art director and print maker, Shane O'Driscoll. This summer we learned how to be editors, friends and work colleagues and we are still learning and admitting it when we have underestimated response times or have been flummoxed by administrative gremlins. As writers ourselves, we understand the waxing and waning of the publishing process and the toil involved in carving a place for your work to sit in an over-saturated landscape and that is why we took our time and gave each piece the consideration it deserved. We are so grateful to have had the support of our funders, patrons, guest contributors and well-wishers in helping us to set up the journal and we recognise every single person who has helped this issue come into being. We remain humbled by your support and hope that you enjoy what we have curated with your good faith.

Lucy, Patrick, Steve and Rosie

Grand So

by Jan Carson

Nobody wants to buy luxury jam.

This is Northern Ireland. In the eighties. People have other things on their minds.

Granda and Granny have tried everything. Advertisements in the paper. An ad on Downtown Radio. A big sign next to the Banbridge turn off – *Loughbrickland Country Preserves* written in curly letters next to a photo of wee pig-tailed Ruth, nibbling strawberry jam off a spoon. When the sign first went up, Ruth hadn't minded being famous. Now she's older, she's mortified. She's for the Academy in September. Every morning and afternoon the school bus will trundle past her big, jammy face.

The car is Granda's latest idea. Granny will drive around with samples, rooting out potential customers. She'll target small shops in villages where the bus only stops twice a day. She'll be covering the whole province: Newry to Ballycastle, Donaghadee to Beleek. Coast to border. Border to coast. Skirting Lough Neagh's dismal shoreline. Circumnavigating Fermanagh's Lakes. Through the moss green Glens of Antrim. Round the skirt tails of the Mournes. Four or five hundred miles per week. She couldn't manage without a car.

It's not the best time to be sending your wife out 'round the country, on her own. There are army boys concealed in hedges, regular checkpoints and ambushes. It's not uncommon to come across a burnt-out car smouldering on the roadside. There's a bomb on the news nearly every night. Granny and Granda don't have a choice. They've thrown everything into the jam. Their savings. The house. The money set aside for Ruth's education. Every bloody penny they have. Granda says it'll be grand. Loughbrickland Country Preserves is just going through a sticky patch. He tries to make a joke of this. *Sticky, ha ha, like the jam.* Ruth can tell he's nervous. He isn't laughing with his eyes. If they want to hold unto the business, Granny needs to find new customers.

Granny's up for the challenge. 'You know me,' she says, 'I could sell snow to the Eskimos.'

'Never worry about the Eskimos,' says Granda. 'It's shifting marmalade to Ulstermen that'll get us out of this hole.'

Granda finds a motor for Granny in the Autotrader. An absolute gem of a car. Ten years old. In decent nick. Two previous owners. Cash in hand. He takes the bus over to Lisburn to pick it up. There is a man in the backseat of the car.

Ruth spots him as soon as Granda pulls into the yard. He's a largish fella of farmer build. He wears reading glasses and a funeral suit. What remains of his hair is grey and swept across a gummy bald spot. It forms a kind of hairy flap. Ruth assumes her granda's given the man a lift though it's odd that he's sitting in the backseat. It looks like he's being chauffeured around.

She waits for the stranger to emerge. He doesn't move. Granda hops out, leaving him there.

'Get in, Marlene,' he says. 'Take her a wee run round the yard. She's a nice-looking motor, isn't she? Only thirty thousand on the clock.'

Granny squeezes her substantial thighs in beneath the wheel. She doesn't acknowledge the man in the back. She places her hands at ten to two, turns the key and revs the engine cautiously.

'Aye, she'll do rightly,' she announces. She pauses then and sniffs the air. 'It fairly stinks in here.' She glances over her shoulder, straight at the man who's lighting his next cigarette off the last. She looks right through him like he isn't there. 'The last owner must've been a smoker. With second-hand motors you should always ask. You cannae shift the smell of fags.'

Granda has asked no such thing. Nor has he checked for the presence of a spare tyre or if the electric windows actually work. (There isn't one, and they don't). The Autotrader's also failed to mention that this 1982 Sierra in Polaris Grey comes complete with the original owner, now deceased. This extra information would hardly have deterred Granda. The same man cannot pass a bargain by. He once returned from Nutts Corner market with three hundred dishwasher tablets bought for two quid. They hadn't owned a dishwasher, or planned to acquire one, but he'd been pleased with his purchase – *proud as punch* – because dishwasher tablets were '*dear enough*'.

The new car does 55 miles to the gallon. This is almost miraculous. What's more, Granda's managed to negotiate twenty quid off the asking price. It's a bargain in his book. If Granny ever thought to complain about taxiing a dead fella around, he'd simply dismiss her concerns, '*you're under no pressure to make friends with him, Marlene. Just you concentrate on the driving. Leave your man to get on with being dead.*' Granny's not for complaining though. Ruth's the only one who can see the Backseat Man. They say weans are more susceptible to things unseen and Ruth's a particularly dreamy kind of wean.

It is mid-July when the car arrives. School is out for another six weeks. Granny won't hear tell of leaving Ruth alone. And Granda spends his days in the shed. He has to keep an eye on the jam as it boils and bubbles inside the huge vats. It cannot be allowed to burn. Money's that tight, a single lost batch could be the straw that breaks the camel's back. Granda hasn't time to mind a child. Ruth offers several alternative options. She could go to Lyndsey's across the field. Lyndsey has six wee brothers and sisters. Her mother won't notice another child. Or there's cousins with a caravan up in Portrush. They're always offering to take Ruth for a couple of weeks. Or the Holiday Bible Club in the Presbyterian. Ruth's not that interested in getting saved, but she could fake it rightly for a week or two.

'No,' says Granny, 'you're coming in the car with me.' And that's her final word on the matter. There's no point trying to negotiate.

Ruth wonders if Granny's always been this strict. It's likely just since Mummy died. A thing like that would make you clingy. You'd be feared of losing anyone else. Ruth was only three when it happened. She has forgotten the time before. She remembers Mummy from photographs. Granny and Granda don't talk about her. Ruth can't even remember what her Mummy's voice sounded like.

The pair of them leave the farm before eight every morning. To speed things up Granny makes their sandwiches the night before. Ruth prefers cheese or ham. If it's tomato, the bread'll be mush long before lunchtime. If it's tuna, it's even worse. The Backseat Man is always waiting for them. He dozes across the length of the seat, his big knees triangled up in the air. When he hears Granny fumbling with her keys he springs up into a sitting position, occupying the space behind the driver's seat. Ruth only needs to turn her head slightly to see him. They're barely down the lane before he's lighting his first cigarette.

The Backseat Man smokes like a chimney. Ruth sometimes wonders if it was the smoking that killed him. She'd ask, but she doesn't want to annoy him further. When she catches his eye in the rear-view mirror, he's always glaring. At her. At Granny. At the telegraph poles, the dry-stone walls and straggly hedges which go swimming past the windscreen. He looks like Granda when the Postman delivers another bank letter. Like he's taken a mouthful of vinegar. Ruth can't get a name out of him. Nor where he's from.

Nor how he wound up here, in the back seat of her granny's car. He's not what you'd call a chatty man.

The first day Ruth fairly batters him with questions. They're up Ballymena direction, flitting through the surrounding villages: Ahoghill, Cullybackey, Kells, Broughshane. Granny says the people in Broughshane have an awful notion of themselves. They've plastered the place in fancy flowers. She parks the car outside a shop. Every available ledge and container is spewing primary-coloured begonias. You can't even see the sign to tell whether it's a Spar or VG. Granny leaves the radio on for Ruth. 'I'll not be more than twenty minutes,' she says. 'Whatever you do, don't leave the car.' Ruth gets out her library book. She watches Granny disappear through a curtain of Barbie pink begonias, clutching her samples and a Tupperware full of pre-cut wheaten squares. She doesn't want to seem uncouth, offering potential customers luxury jam off a teaspoon.

Alone, at last with the Backseat Man, Ruth sets the library book aside and begins her interrogation. *What's your name? Where do you come from? What's it like being dead? Have you been to Heaven? Was it nice up there? Could you have a wee look about for my mummy; she got killed in a bomb, a few years back? Angela Kelly is her name.* All credit to him, his face softens a little hearing this. But does he answer Ruth's questions? He does not. He holds his silence like a riot shield, smoking one curt cigarette after the other whilst Ruth continues to pitch questions at him. It is only when she asks if the Sierra used to be his car, that the Backseat Man finally opens his mouth. 'Jesus, Mary and Joseph you've some nerve wee lassie,' he says, 'it's still my bloody car.' Ruth notes the language – *bad* – and the accent – *Newry* – and understands they've been landed with the *other sort* of ghost.

Later that week, in Rasharkin, her suspicions are confirmed. Granny pulls in to let a combine pass and, noticing they're outside a chapel, the Backseat Man crosses himself. *Spectacles, testicles, wallet and watch.* Ruth's heard this off the wee lads in school. This is the first time she's seen anybody do it for real. There are no Catholics in her world. She's not a baby. She knows they exist. It was the Catholics who blew up her mummy; not for any particular reason, save being in the wrong place at the wrong time. Ruth knows the difference between their lot and hers. They fly a green, white and orange flag and paint your man with Jesus hair on their walls. *Bobby what's-his-name that died.* They have crosses on their church roofs and Mary in a box by the gate. Ruth's lot fly the Union Jack and have the Queen or curly King Billy on their walls. They paint their kerbs red, white and blue; a fresh lick of paint every year for the Twelfth.

Ruth keeps track of the differences as they drive around, labelling the places in her head. Dunloy is Catholic. Comber, Protestant. Fintona's Catholic. Holywood's too posh to tell. Ruth worries about Granny going into certain shops. Wrong time, wrong place and anything could happen. Surely Granny must know this more than most. When Ruth asks if it's sensible, selling jam to Catholics, Granny tries to laugh it off. 'Jam's jam,' she says, 'I'll be grand, my Love. Nobody can tell which foot I kick with. A name like Kelly goes either way.'

There are other things which go both ways. Not football, obviously. If somebody's in a Celtic top, you can tell straight away they're not like you. The same goes for schools and where you live. Also, where you buy your groceries. Granny says Stewarts is a Protestant outfit – even the carrier bags are loyal orange. Crazy Prices is for the other lot. 'You can tell from the look of it,' she says, 'the food's just flung at the shelves.'

Jam is not sectarian. It's equally popular with both sides; like dogs and shell suits and that woman, from here, who won the Olympics and always gets asked to open things. Ruth is beginning to wonder if country music might be the same. Country and Western's all they listen to at home. They make the switch to Country Gospel on Sunday's because Sunday is Jesus' day. Granny's a great one for John Denver. She's also partial to Tammy Wynette. She keeps an old shoe box of cassettes tucked beneath the passenger seat. It's Ruth's job to flip them over when the side runs out. Ruth's also expected to harmonise when Granny's in the mood for singing along.

The Backseat Man is a Country fan too. He nods along to Rhinestone Cowboy. He taps his finger on the back of the headrest while Tammy's whining her way through D.I.V.O.R.C.E. Ruth feels the vibrations, like Morse code twitching at the back of her head. The next time Granny leaves them alone, the Backseat Man asks if there's any Kris Kristofferson under the seat. It's the first time he's tried to start a chat. Even though Ruth's never heard of this Kristoff man and is certain sure he's not in the shoebox, she tries to keep the conversation going.

'Do you like country music?' she asks.

'Aye,' the Backseat Man replies.

'So does Granny.'

'Aye, I can see that,' says the man.

She's about to elaborate when Granny returns with an orange ice pop for Ruth and a tin of Lilt for herself. Ruth is dying to ask the Backseat Man what he was doing listening to Country and Western. On the telly, Catholics only ever listen to twiddly diddly music, fiddles and whistles and wee flat drums; the sort of music folks danced to in the olden days. Ruth's always assumed Country's just for Protestants. She wonders if the Backseat Man got himself killed for listening to it. Stranger things have happened here. Like, this lad she knows from Young Farmers'; he got beat up for walking past a Catholic pub in an orange t-shirt. Sometimes when Granda's watching the news, he'll mumble in a sad, sort of weary voice, 'boys a boys, they're killing each other over nothing these days.'

Granda worries. Especially when Granny's out in the car. He'll start to panic if they're even a few minutes late home. He keeps the 10ps from his change and presents them to Granny every Monday morning. She stores them in a Flora tub inside the glove compartment. Every hour or so she'll pull up at a phone box and hand one to Ruth. It's her job to call home.

Banbridge 43157.

'We're in Annahilt,' she'll say, or 'Strabane,' or, 'Comber,' depending on where they're at. 'We're fine. We'll be home at the usual time.'

'Grand so,' Granda will say.

Ruth can always hear the relief in his voice; a slow exhalation, like the morning mist rising, as he hangs up the phone and returns to his jam.

If there's more than two hours between calls, Granny starts to get twitchetty. Granda'll be going up the walls. 'Keep a wee eye out for a phone box, Love,' she'll say. Ruth's the best at spotting them. She likes to feel like she's helping Granny. She likes having a job to do. It's why she always volunteers to do the dishes. And takes out the bin on Tuesday mornings. And cleans her own room without being asked. Nobody's ever said anything, but Ruth knows she owes her grandparents a lot. In films when your mummy dies and your da's not around, you get sent to a children's home. Though it's an odd sort of set up – living with a pair of old ones – Ruth feels lucky to have a family.

She wonders about the Backseat Man. *Does he have a family? Maybe a wee lassie of his own? Are there folks out there missing him since he died?* She observes his face in the rear-view mirror. He doesn't look like a family man. There's no softness to him. His mouth has forgotten how to smile. She can't imagine him talking to children or puckering up those thin pink lips to plant a bedtime kiss on some wee girl's cheek. Still, she asks him anyway. Thursday morning, in a layby somewhere on the edge of Larne. Granny's gone off to spend a penny, leaving the two of them alone. Ruth lowers her voice to infer concern.

She doesn't anticipate hysterics – he doesn't seem like an emotional man – but you never know how folks are feeling deep inside. Granny's not a weepy woman but Ruth has twice caught her sobbing over Mummy's school photograph.

'So,' she says, 'turning round in her seat to meet his eye, do you… I mean, did you have a family yourself?'

The Backseat Man takes a long draw on his cigarette and exhales slowly. The smoke catches at the back of Ruth's throat. She struggles not to cough.

'Everybody has a family,' he says.

'Yeah, but were you close to yours?' she asks.

'I wouldn't say close,' says the Backseat Man. 'But I wasn't bad to them.' He pauses then, tapping his cigarette on the open window, to dispense a dollop of ash. 'I wouldn't be bad to anyone.'

This proves to be the longest conversation of their mutual acquaintance. Ruth understands the significance of what's been said. It has the feel of a confession though she's only ever seen them done on TV. The Backseat Man would not be bad to *anyone*. There's a whole world of wideness in that one wee word.

It is still hanging in the clammy air when Granny returns to the car, cleaning her hands with a fresh wet wipe. Ruth wants to ask the Backseat Man what he means. *Does his anyone extend to her? What about the rest of her lot? If you weren't bad to anyone, did this eventually make you good?* Ruth chances another look in the rear-view mirror. The Backseat Man has leant his forehead against the window. His eyes are trained on the hard shoulder as it goes screeching by. In profile he looks furious. Like somebody you'd see guldering from a platform on the news. It is hard to imagine much good in him.

Granny's fairly trucking today. She insists upon eating their ham sandwiches in transit. Ruth fills the tea mug from the big thermos flask. They pass it backwards and forwards over the gearstick, trying to contain the manic slurp as the car jolts over potholes and muddy ruts. It's mostly back roads this afternoon. One-car-at-a-time numbers with hedges so high, no part of the road lies outside the shadow. They're visiting all the wee villages around Newry – Warrenpoint, Rathfriland, Camlough – flirting with the snaked line of the border; never daring to cross.

Ruth peers into the distance, imagining it will look different in the South. It appears to be exactly the same. Green fields. Bungalows. Scraggly patches of forest trees. This surprises her. Granny describes it differently. She has a horror of the Free State. A friend's sister once holidayed in Sligo, northern plates on full display. All four of her tyres were slashed as she slept in a caravan just ten feet from the car. The implication being, she should count herself lucky she wasn't killed. Or worse. Granny likes to tell this story and other similar stories of hapless Northerners punished for naïvely assuming the South to be safe.

Twice Ruth glimpses the border at the end of a road. Twice Granny curses and stalls the car as she turns. She's normally a very capable driver. Ruth's never been over the border before, but she recognises it from the TV news: the breeze-block towers and barriers like dropped arms scraping the asphalt, the young soldiers lying in ditches with guns, all the ordinary cars, engines idling as they worm their way south. This is bandit country, or so Granda says. It's a place where people disappear. Ruth knows not to say anything 'til they're a good mile away, heading in the right direction again.

An anxious silence has crept into the car. She feels the pressure of it pinching her forehead like a too tight hat. Granny hunched over the steering wheel. The Backseat Man glaring at the back of her head. Ruth turns the stereo on, not really caring what music comes out, only wanting noise to ease the silence. It's Glen Campbell: *Wichita Lineman*. Everyone likes Glen Campbell, even the Backseat Man. But Granny barely lets him get a half sentence out before flicking the stereo off. 'Not today,' she says. 'I can't be doing with any distractions.'

They are somewhere between Mullaghbawn and Crossmaglen when the Backseat Man leans over and taps Ruth on the shoulder. In the strained silence, she's almost forgotten he's back there. All her nerves rush to the point where his hand has made contact with her shoulder. His touch is cold, then hot like freezer burn. It seeps through the fabric of Ruth's polo shirt. She shivers, though it's stifling behind the glass.

'Don't go down the next road,' the Backseat Man says.

'What's that?' asks Ruth. The words are out before she can stop them.

'I didn't say anything,' Granny replies.

'Sorry, I thought I heard something outside.'

Ruth catches his eye in the rear-view mirror. She tries to frame a question with her face.

'Make her stop,' the man says. Ruth can tell he really means it.

'Stop the car,' she says.

'I'm not stopping out here, in the middle of nowhere.'

'Please, Granny, you need to stop.'

'Why?'

'I'm going to boke,' says Ruth. She clamps a hand across her mouth, bugging her pale, blue eyes out dramatically.

'For goodness sake, Child. You pick your moments.'

Granny pulls off the road, running two wheels up the side of the verge so it comes to rest at a skewiff angle. Ruth leaps from the passenger side. She clambers up the verge and leans out over the prickly, green hedge. She tries to look like she's being sick. She glances backwards to make sure Granny's buying this charade. Granny is fixing her lipstick in the mirror: drawing the wide O of her lips into a tight pucker then dragging the edges out into a thin red gash. Even from this distance Ruth can see the red lipstick is too bright for a woman of Granny's age. The Backseat Man catches Ruth staring. He gestures with his cigarette hand, making tight, fire-lit loops, as if to say, *keep it up a bit longer.*

Ruth thrusts her head over the hedge. She makes a series of exaggerated puking noises. Two black and white cows dander over. They stand in front of her, staring, damp-eyed. In the distance a tractor makes slow, chugging progress across the horizon. Ruth hasn't a baldy notion where she is. This could be any field in Ulster. It's the same view she sees every morning when she opens the curtains in her bedroom. Her teacher claims Ireland has forty shades of green. In the North the palette's limited. Half a dozen shades of pine and myrtle form the spectrum of her world. This is all Ruth's ever known: hedges, peat moss, farmer's fields and twice a year – if she's lucky – a run up to Newcastle just to check the sea's still there. She went to Belfast once on a nursery school trip to the panto. That was before her mummy died. There's no way Granda would let her go up to the city after that. In the city there are always bombs.

Ruth counts to sixty. Then counts to sixty once again. It's a trick for marking a minute, *one thousand, two thousand, three thousand* and so on. It's almost three minutes since she left the car. She's just about to turn and walk back to the passenger seat when, in the distance, very close, a noise rises up like drums and guns. Ruth feels the sick thud of it in her belly. Her bones understand what it is.

Up comes the bile and the vomit. This time for real. She misses the field, misses the hedge, watches helpless as it splatters over her shoes and socks. In the field a hundred thousand previously hidden birds rise from the grass and bordering hedges like raindrops returning to the clouds. When Ruth turns back to the car, Granny is already out and scrambling up the verge to grab her, vomitty socks and all. Her lipstick has slid in the blast, leaving a long red gash across her cheeks.

She is crying and laughing and falling over.

She is saying, 'oh my God. Oh my God. Oh my God.' And it doesn't sound like a curse so much as a thing you'd hear in church, sung by a choir.

Afterwards the Backseat Man is gone.

They don't even bother to look for a phone box, they just find the nearest respectable looking house and ask to use the telephone. When Granda comes on the phone Granny says, 'we're fine, Love. We're both fine. But, if Ruth hadn't...' and then she can't get any words out. So, Ruth takes the phone out of her hand and says, 'we're fine, Granda. We're on our way home now. See you later.' She waits for Granda to say, 'grand so,' but there's nothing but silence on the end of the line. Even though she's pure sobbing, and probably isn't fit to drive, Granny still remembers to give the lady twenty pence for using the phone.

Once they're on the other side of Newry, on the dual carriageway heading home, Ruth asks if they can listen to Johnny Cash. Granny says, 'anything you want, wee Pet,' and turns the radio on. Their voices are like water trembling, but they still manage to sing a bit of 'Ring of Fire.'

Ruth sings loud, so loud there isn't any room to think.

The man in the backseat never returns.

disrepair

by Eniola Abdulroqeeb Arówóló

mother, where are you? a boy says before a bomb

                              strips off his flesh to seduce the evening crows.

i am what this country made me — a wounded tulip.

                    the other day in Sokoto, a mob undid a girl to please God.

how wild we are to justice despite all that has burned through us.

                    why don't you write happy poems? my lover asked.

what nectar can a grapefruit grant a sour tongue?

                    believe me when i say the fire burns in me each day

like a sea waylaid by tempest.

                    & i don't want to wilt before i bear all my fruits. yet, the soil

is infertile — rusting glory. i pray to find home,

                    a vineyard of ripe laughter. i wake

with charred little bodies.

                    tonight, i morph into a bad tune from this cello. the herons
are dead.

Fiery Dawn

by James Harris

mortality
— an excerpt from *The Flaw Memoirs*

by Nidhi Zak / Aria Eipe

You could be forgiven for thinking that my father only ever wanted one thing, more than anything – that the women he loved would not die while he was away. But life can be cruel like that, thwarting our only desires. Both his mother and his wife would choose to leave when he had already left them

understand – I say this as if it is his fault, but do I not also run? Do I not know the intimacy of this impulse, bladder-voiding-rush of this urge(ncy), when all my limbs feel on the verge of fleeing, into cardinal direction, cardinal sin – Dear Father. Am I not similarly seduced into the fugitive?

My grandmother, at 92, bedridden and beautiful, is labouring to breathe. She rasps, a sound not unlike our cat hacking up a hairball. I pick up, with only half of my heart, the plastic mouth of the mask. At 19, I have my own notions about prolonging life. I am wedded to the natural, to letting things happen in their own rhythm, to letting go. My father has other ideas, of course, which is why the apparatus, the oxygen, the stuff of drowning divers. I know the drill here, I must cover her mouth, resuscitate her, force the air back into her tired lungs. But this time my grandmother stops me, clasping my hand with a strength that arrests me. All her life hauling buckets, running hoes, pulling weeds – why am I surprised? She shakes her head, this woman, always so firm. I hang the mask back on its hook. I sit close to her, look into her eyes which are also my eyes, her once-brown iris now a fluid, limpid, gullfeathergrey. She gazes at me through this radiant fog of perception. She loosens her hold.

I watch her breath make its final slow lap through the waters of her leaving, moving, like grace, through the very last of her, battered body. Years later, in a desert land, a whistle will pierce its way through the wind and I will feel it again – this harbinger encircling my wrist, the death grip of certainty, the weight of a hawk on my hand. Whatever I will learn of death, I know, I will learn it now, forever.

forgotten
— an excerpt from *The Flaw Memoirs*
by Nidhi Zak / Aria Eipe

I have worked myself up into a state over my most recent heartbreak. I am staying with one of my oldest friends on the bluest edge of Maine, where we spent four years studying for a liberal arts degree. She has driven out, with the dog, on an errand – so I find myself alone among the pine and kelp. I want to speak with a man who loves me, and who is not my father, but no one comes to mind. I would have called my ex-husband, but he has blocked me on every available communication channel. In a fit of something, I consider erasing all his contact details from my digital storage. I will always recall his email, of course, but I realise that I have actually forgotten his phone number.

This is not as terrible as it sounds, for, because of the way phones work now, I never really had to commit it to memory – and anyway, it was a new number that he only had for a year, the same time in which we were drifting apart. Maybe my mind had an inkling of foreshadowing and didn't think to go to the trouble. But there is one number I do recall, that's branded into my memory, even now, fifteen years later. My first crush in America. My first affair. A married man. Whose number I would not make permanent in my device because he'd always say: *this is the last time, we can't keep doing this*. But we kept doing this.

I stare at the slim, flat rectangle in my hand. I watch my thumb dial the familiar configuration – first digits all on the right, the rest dead centre. It rings four, five times, goes to voicemail. I hesitate after the beep, then say, 'Hey [   ], it's me. It's been a while, you're probably not even at this number anymore. I'm in Maine, I'm… looking for the person I used to be. I wonder if we could talk.' I stare at the phone again. I hang up.

Not a few minutes after, I get a text. When I hear the notification, it makes me thrill a little, curiously, the same way I used to when I got one of those illicit – let's meet [here] in a few [hours] – messages from him, those days.

Hi. You just called this number and left a message.

I don't think I'm the person you are looking for.

I'm sorry.

15:35

I know it's him, because of the tone, the way he writes in full sentences with full stops, how he is not of a generation that instinctively relies on emoticons and shorthand, the careful ambiguous words that neither confirm nor deny. But mostly, I know, because there is something in the body that does not forget a lover's language.

Later, I text him back:

Thank you, for the message, and for your kindness.
It was a long time ago, but I thought I'd try.
Wishing you every good thing :)

19:48

You as well :) good luck with everything.

19:49

Dreams of Fish

by Mark Thomas

In conclusion, fish dreams can be summed up in two ways:

Positive *fish dreams often indicate that you are ready to step forward with creative opportunities, you have natural curiosity, are emotionally mature, and always see new possibilities.*

Negative *fish dreams often suggest abandoned ideas, doubt, creative blocks, emotional immaturity, or spiritual stagnation.*

I dreamed of fish again.

The environment was the same as always, a flooded suburban neighborhood, very similar to the place where I grew up. There were no recognizable buildings or landmarks, but the wide grassy lots and deep ditches lining the streets were very familiar.

Crystal-clear water inundated a low-lying neighbor's yard, creating an artificial lake several feet deep. The grass was long like seaweed and waved back and forth, buffeted by invisible currents. The fish, chunky and white, schooled above the heaving lawn with their noses all facing left.

It was difficult to identify the species. They weren't needle-shaped like pike, they didn't have distinct lateral lines like bass, they were the wrong color for carp or perch. If an insane zoologist held a fillet knife to my throat, demanding a taxonomy, I'd have to say they were mutant utlip innows.

In reality, cutlips are tiny things, perhaps three inches long, delicate pieces of iridescent jewelry, manufactured in a Tiffany workshop under the sea. The behemoths in my dream were at least three feet long but they did have similar facial expressions. Their bright white cheeks and throats framed oversized black eyes with pupils that tried to look everywhere at once. The fish seemed puzzled by their strange dream-environment and perhaps suspected that something was amiss. They had relatively small mouths, lips pursed with disapproval, and their cheeks vibrated as if they were desperately trying to make sense of this new world by speed-tasting it.

I was relatively young in this latest dream, although my exact age was indeterminate.

Sometimes I seemed like a child, proudly stomping around a wet yard in new boots, but other times I was clearly old enough to drive and weighed down by vague responsibilities.

Nothing much happened in the dream. I wanted to catch the fish but couldn't because there was always some problem with my tackle. The line was snarled, the rod tip was broken, the lures slipped through my fingers like real fish. I tried to problem-solve, but my fumbling movements were too slow. Strangely enough, I wasn't frustrated because I was aware that I was dreaming and understood that dream-movements are often defined by clear-jelly clumsiness.

Anyway, I couldn't hang around the neighborhood not-catching fish, I had to leave for some important appointment so I jumped behind the wheel of a car. As I drove past a network of deep, flooded ditches, I saw more fish pooled in front of culverts. They were staring at the dark openings and politely waving their tails. Their very presence was tantalizing and I couldn't wait to come back, when I had more time to catch them. I narrowly avoided a head-on collision with another distracted driver who was staring at the ditch-fish as well.

That evening, I visited friends, a couple who happened to be newly married. They gave me tea and pastries, using the dishes I gave them as a wedding present. While we were eating, I described my dream and asked, 'What do you think it means?'

The woman sipped at her tea and said, 'It's obvious. You're pathologically lonely. Fish cluster together in schools, but you're all by yourself in the dream. You wish you were part of a larger group.' Her lips pursed together and her expression was eerily similar to that of the cutlip minnows in my dream, except she seemed self-satisfied, rather than worried or puzzled.

In some circles, it's probably considered impolite for a host to point out that a guest's life is empty, but we weren't exactly strangers. The woman and I had known each other for years and even dated, briefly, just before her marriage. There was no cruelty in her declaration, just the usual confident smugness that happy people can't control.

Her husband was in the kitchenette, chopping up fruit for another dessert. He shook his head at his wife's assessment and said, "No, that's not it at all. Fish have a very, very specific meaning when they appear in dreams."

We both looked at him. I wasn't aware that dream images could be treated like parts of a mathematical equation: $X=8$, $Y=11$. I thought nocturnal messaging was *supposed* to be fuzzy.

The man paused, letting tension build, then he smiled broadly, amused at our ignorance. "Fish have always been associated with sperm, in dreams." He pointed the knife at me. "If you were a woman, it would mean you were worried about being pregnant. Since you're a man, it obviously means you're wondering if you might have impregnated someone."

The woman coughed out a mouthful of tea and her shoulders hunched up like gill plates.

I put down my cup, which rattled onto its saucer. I was suddenly embarrassed by the freshman-psych imagery of my dream: culverts and ditches and hair-grass and wriggling white creatures. I don't know why the puerile Freudian implications weren't obvious when I woke up this morning.

"You may be right, in theory," I said, the words sounding light and dismissive. "But in my case, your interpretation is impossible; I simply don't have anyone to spawn with."

There was a pause, then we all laughed at the silly euphemism and the man resumed his chopping.

Nevertheless, it was an awkward exchange, and I left as soon as I could, after the pavlova.

That night, I dreamed of fish again.

gramática
by Leah Duarte

(i)

eu tive tantas saudades tuas   i missed you so much

(ii)

if you translate word by word   i had so many [*saudades*] of yours

eu tenho saudades   i miss [something]

word by word   i have [something]   *saudade* is generous that way

(iii)

it's *a festa de são joão* the tables are heaving with dessert chocolate mousse so thick you can hang your spoon upside down a bowl of cherries in water to keep them cool hands snatching profiteroles stuffed with whipped cream and egg yolk and sugar a dozen just for you filled with *natas* no *ovos moles* because you can't stand them baby of the party they'll spoil you until your stomach hurts   until you can't hear yourself over their laughter, the sun-soaked pleasure of it reverberating through three generations you used to think the most beautiful songs from this country were about mourning someone's mother pets your hair   *linda menina*   beautiful girl   someone's daughter fills your plate again   there's so much left over that two neighbours' fridges have to be borrowed just to fit it all later you will wonder at the kind of friendship that is an open door now you catch the mousse as it's passed over the fence and scurry laughing into a stranger's house try to find space stack bowls and plates cross fingers that plastic wrapped *natas do ceu* can hold a plastic bowl of strawberries   cream from heaven make us a miracle because there's no room left   *tu tens saudades* you have [a caved-in pavlova in your hands] they made it because it's your favourite the strawberries are dissolving the meringue where they touch the whole plate is sugar-sticky even the bottom   more food to bring up off the table   you're alone with yourself for the first time all day baby of the party you never knew you wanted tables groaning with food and love and sun-browned elbows until this moment   *vê la se tu percebes, menina*   try to understand   this is going to end this is not yours baby of the party *uma convidada* is still only a guest baby of the party you cannot transmute your translations baby of the party this is not your family   someone laughs   distant   the sugar itches your empty palms as it dries

(iv)

tu vais ter saudades   you will miss this   something of this will be left behind inside of you

(v)

tu já estás a ter saudades   you are already missing this   your body has already made space for this absence   you'll need more   *saudade* is generous that way   *saudade* propagates   you will take it back across the ocean with you   an invasive species already adolescent around your ribs

(vi)

the party is still going   *tu já estás a ter saudades*   warm hands pressing your hands your face *estás tão linda, meu amor*   word by word   you are so beautiful   my love

Ireland's First Serial Killer

by Dean Fee

The first letter came with the second post of the day. The envelope was smattered with fat raindrops that spiked out like a child's drawing of the sun and on it was written, Garda Barracks, Barracks Street.

There was no stamp.

The Inspector ripped the narrow end open with a thumb, blew inside and pulled the paper out and unfolded it. Written on it in scrawling, coloured crayons were the words: We did old Mrs Murtagh and she won't be the last.

Eileen Murtagh, a widowed woman who lived in one of the old council houses up the back of town, had died unexpectantly only two days before. The medical report had said it was a brain aneurysm, a hereditary thing most likely, since her brother and both her parents had gone the same way. The other possible cause was trauma, and God knew there was plenty of that to go around. The one thing Inspector Stack knew was, it wasn't a bloody murder.

His name was John Stack and he was a well-feared, and therefore, well-respected man where he came from. Religious by nurture, he owed all he had to the man above and he thanked him day and night. Penitential kneeling before his bed by the darkened window, hands flat together, his bristling lips muttering the same prayers he'd had slapped into him as a child. In the bright of day, he rubbed a holy medal his nephew had brought back from the Vatican City and counted each of his blessings twice. Thank God for me mother, he'd say. Thank God for her. And me brother and his wee ones and their health. Thank God for them. Thank God for the day that's in it, rain or shine, it's great to be alive. Thank God for the work, for God himself knows there's work to be done on this island where the people have lost their faith in droves. He thanked God for everything and claimed nothing for himself.

He was from the sea and of the sea but found himself now marooned in a world of lakes and woods. Old bog roads gravelled over, avenues of loose chippings signs. They had said he was getting old. They said the times were moving forward out here by the water. It was youth they wanted now, a more relatable voice for the young ones coming up. So put out to pasture he was. To some backward town bang in the middle of the island. A place where he might be put to use, they said. He hadn't much excuse not to go, so off he went, three sheets to the wind, his little holy medal reddening his thumb as the bus shuttled him around windy roads to the dark depths of the midlands. The town itself had no name other than The Town. It was once a tiny one-street thing, with a shop and a butchers and three pubs, but as industry came and went, factories were built, and with them great sprawling housing estates. Houses sprung up from the ground, pebble-dashed or skimmed grey, the mounds of their excavation left mountainous beside them like sleeping sentinels. Families were moved in without so much as a curtain hung up and their lives played out under bare bulbs and the flicker of the TV. New roads were lain down, tarmacadam still wet when the wheels of motors tore down them in the early mornings.

Then one day construction stopped. Houses were left without roofs or windows, or even families because the work was followed east or west, north or south. The few that remained were pocketed amidst ghostly grey blocks, buildings with eyes that followed as you walked the unfinished path to the gardenless houses that had promised so much.

Inspector Stack wasn't well liked in the town's barracks. Not one of the other men had reached a rank above the basic Garda, and the Inspector's apparent care for climbing the ladder, his desire to do actual police work, lead them to mock him. Behind his back they called him The Sheriff. They would take on his lame walk and mime counting rosary beads in fervent prayer.

When the second letter came it was one of them who had opened it. Again, it was a slip of paper with the same address, no stamp, and the message was written in crayon. The guards all huddle around to read it: We ran Martin McMenamin off the road. There'll be another in a week.

Marty Mack? said one guard.

Aye, said another.

Sure that was a car crash.

Marty was hammered at the wheel, said a third.

When was he not hammered at the wheel?

Then what the fuck is this lad on about?

Lads, not lad.

Wha?

It's not just one lad. It's lads. Look, and with a big finger pointed to the first word: we.

Someone said they better show the Sheriff, and in quiet hierarchal fashion, they stepped away, leaving the runt of the litter, Paul Óg to deal with it.

When the Inspector came back later that afternoon, Paul Óg approached, the sheet of paper trembling in his hands. Though they mocked the Inspector, they were not wholly stupid, they knew what sort of man he was. Holy up onto a point, he wouldn't be long giving you the back of his hand, or worse, the front end of that old Smith and Wesson he kept in his drawer.

What is it, so? said the Inspector without looking up.

There's been a letter, sir, said Paul Óg.

Oh yeah? For who?

Well, it doesn't actually say for who, but for you, I suppose.

The Inspector knew he wasn't liked, and he liked it that way. If he was going to have to spend the rest of his days trying to wrangle these God-forsaken fools, then it was better if they didn't get too friendly.

For the love of God, man. Will you spit it out?

A ripple of laughter from the rest, shot down by the Inspector's glare.

Paul Óg reached across the desk, the paper hanging limp from his hand, and the Inspector took it. He read it and sighed the deep sigh of the defeated. Christ, he said. When did this come? Where's the envelope? For fuck's sake man, get the envelope.

It wasn't long before the town heard about the letters. The men who worked as guards here, worked first as mouthpieces. Unable to hold their piss, they spouted off about the two letters they had received to anyone who would listen. All had ears for gossip in this town, where the biggest thing that had happened in the last twenty years was the erection of the 4G mast.

The news of the letters brought rumours that the town had a serial killer. In McFadden's – one of the three pubs in town – the locals elbowed the bar and traded suspicions.

Ireland's first, said the butcher Malachy.

First what? said Bats Collins.

Serial killer.

Is that right? said Dan Coote, horsing bacon fries into him like it was his last supper.

That's bollox, said Bats.

It is not, said the butcher. Get it up on that phone there and see for yourself.

You know as well as I know there's no coverage in here.

He has you there, said wee Ollie Door, a wry smile on his pale face.

Ollie was a fry cook who worked in a chipvan halfway between here and another place. He and Bats were old friends, since they were kids. There were in their mid-twenties but since they were the only two bucks who had not left town after finishing school, they were still seen as pups. All the men around them were nearing fifty and loved to wind Bats up.

Bats was a volatile wee fucker. A low self-esteem passed down to him by his father, lead him to take umbrage against anyone who looked sideways at him. He was all talk, posturing, chest out, top pulled off. An act that would usually see him escorted away promising severe retribution.

Ollie, on the other hand, was a quiet sort of chap, not a bad bone in his body. But he was worse than Bats in one way. He was easily led.

Who do you reckon it is, then? said Eamon Collins, the Local Businessman. My money is on Podge Rogers. There's something not right with that wee prick.

All the men nodded in consideration.

Might be, they said. Could be him.

Wouldn't put it past him after hearing what he did all those years ago.

What did he do? said Bats.

Ah, said the butcher, waving his hand. That's all in the past now. He's already gotten his punishment for that. And besides, there's no way it was Podge. Podge is a wee rat but he's a different kind of rat.

The butcher's proclamation was accepted. Another round was ordered, and the talk moved on to poor School Maura. She was awful sick, and it was only a matter of time.

The day after School Maura died, a week to the day from the last, the third letter came.

We are Ireland's first serial killers, it said. We took Maura O'Hara's life last night and there'll be another next week.

A week later another one. This time the writers claimed to have killed Father Feeney. Now the manner of Father Feeney's death had not been made public knowledge. He had been found by his housekeeper, strung up inside his own wardrobe in the midst of performing an act of auto-erotic asphyxiation. Inspector Stack had been smart enough to keep that little detail out of any mouths that might mouth it, but God knew this town liked to talk. He was sick to the teeth of this whole thing and was going to put a stop to it.

He called a meeting with all his staff. They gathered around the bullpen of desks and watched the Inspector as he rotated on his heels, addressing all at once.

I want a man on the door 24/7 to catch any little gurrier coming by with another one of these letters.

A round of nods.

You, you and you. I want you at the top of main street stopping anyone coming in or out of the town. Ask them every question under the sun. It doesn't matter what the answers are. What we want is to rattle them. Do you understand me?

Nods from the three men spoken to.

We understand, Inspector, they said.

Good – Now. There's a serious issue within this garda station of little mice with big ears and even bigger mouths. Keep them shut until we catch these wee fuckers. Do you hear me? If anyone else dies, God forbid, come straight to me. Don't go telling your mother or her mother, not your wife or your fucking therapist. Me. You tell me. Right?

Right.

Right, dismissed.

As the men went on their way there was the jingle of someone coming in the anteroom door. The Inspector told Paul Óg, who hadn't been given a job, to go entertain the walk-in. Moments later, a knock on his door and Paul Óg's horrible little head.

Sir? he said. It's the butcher Malachy. He says he needs a word.

The Inspector waved him in.

As you'd expect of a butcher, Malachy Mahon was a big man, and though he was in his plain clothes, he still had the hue of blood off him, his skin as raw and pink as a sausage. He stepped sideways into the room and closed the door carefully behind him, his huge fist enveloping the doorknob.

Inspector, he said, and stood in front of the desk. A small word?

The Inspector motioned for him to sit in the chair, but the butcher shook his head. This won't take a minute, he said, the giddy grin of the informant spreading across his face.

That night it pissed rain something serious. Torrential it was. Gusts of wind carried the fat drops sideways across the town, tucking them in under the eaves of houses, thoroughly dousing the entire place. For hours it went on with brief flashes of lighting and rolling rumblings of thunder. It had slackened a little the next morning, become misty, but nonetheless it was ever present and seemed like it always would be.

Talking to the guards through the window of his Subaru, chipvan fry cook, Ollie Door, burst into tears when asked what he might know about a murder. The two guards affecting the stop looked at each other across the car's roof before one said, Would you mind following us into the station, Mr. Door? We have a few questions we'd like to ask you.

Inspector Stack was at his desk when the two men brought Ollie in. He nodded towards the secured room they called The Box and followed after them. Ollie was thrown down into the old plastic chair and told to sit quietly.

And stop fucking crying, will ya?

The Inspector caught the arresting guard's arm. What about the other one? he said. No sign of him?

No, said the guard.

Fuck's sake. Sure wasn't it him the butcher told us was the main man?

The guard agreed but insisted he'd get words out of this young fella. Sure look at him, sir. He's already pissed himself.

It was true, Ollie Door was doubled over sobbing, a dark stain had spread down his leg.

Oi! What have you got there?

Spotting something in Ollie's hands, the Inspector launched himself into the room and onto him. Ollie fought bravely for all of half a second before the phone was wrenched from him.

For fuck sake, Garda, said the Inspector. You didn't think to take the phone off him?

Ah shite, said the guard. Ah fuck.

The Inspector tried to open the phone, but it was password protected.

What have you been sending on this, you wee shite?

Nothing, sir, cried Ollie. I swear.

What's the password? Open it up.

Like a child refusing his greens, Ollie shut his mouth and eyes and shook his head.

The Inspector swore to himself again and then asked the guard if he had at least searched the fucking car.

He hadn't.

In the boot they found the incriminating refill pad and pack of crayons as well as a school bag filled with a clean set of clothes, a rain jacket, a towel, a pack of protein bars, a large tub of cold spaghetti bolognese and an 8-pack of Wagon Wheels.

When the contents of the boot were set down in front of Ollie Door, he burst into tears all over again.

Gonna have a wee picnic in the rain, were we Ollie?

Oh Jesus, he cried. Oh Jesus fuck.

The Inspector came into the room now and sat down in front of him.

You'd want to start talking, young lad.

The woods gave little phone coverage but when a bar did eventually arrive a text came through from Ollie: Arrested, was all it said.

Bats was deep in the forest in an old tepee-like hut that must have been built by children. There were two logs left angled around a ring of rocks with a mound of soaked branches inside it. The thought of lighting a fire occurred to him but the rain was too heavy. It was pouring in through the gaps in the make-shift moss roof and the only thing he could do was huddle into himself. He had texted Ollie earlier to come find him, to bring him a change of clothes and a coat and some food, but that plan was fucked now.

His fingers were numb from the rain and the cold. They were red from the blood.

The butcher should've have kept his mouth shut. It had only been a fucking laugh, just a little joke he had been having with everyone. Like, as if there was actually a serial killer. He hadn't even thought of that until the butcher had said it that night in McFadden's. Before that it was just funny to him to wind that new guard up. Him with the big holy head on him. A man like that, who took himself so seriously, was asking to be messed with.

Bats had been delighted to hear all the craic from Paul Óg in the station every time they received a new letter, but when he told him that the butcher had been in putting words in the new Inspector's ear – well that just made him angry. The intention wasn't to kill him, only frighten him a bit, but one thing lead to another and—

In a red mist Bats had parked a few doors down from the butcher's shop. The torrential rain had only just started, casting main street into an oppressive dull made all the worse by rays of sunshine breaking through clouds away out towards the hills. He kept the radio off but he had the heat on full and it blew about him in a slow suffocating way. He could feel sweat drip cool and ticklish from his oxters and down his sides but he made no move to wipe it. The quiet rage inside him kept him strangely still and he felt that if he moved in any sharpish way he might let something loose that could not be reeled back in. He kept eyes on the glow from the butcher's shop and by half five Malachy Mahon had come out onto the street to reclaim the signs that advertised his deals.

The squeal of the door closing stopped as Bats stuck a foot in the jam.

Batsy, said the butcher, confusion and fear crossing his face. What's the craic?

Bats stepped inside and closed the door. He twisted the key and flipped the sign, so it read *open* on their end, and in the humming white light from the fly catcher, he backed the butcher into a dark corner of his shop.

You've been telling tales, Malachy, said Bats.

I haven't, Bats, said the butcher.

Ah, but you have.

The butcher eyed around him for the knives he had already put away. He saw the wink of light off the blade in Bats' hand and once again insisted on his innocence. Not one word, Batsy. I'm telling ya.

Bats took a deep breath that failed to calm him.

There's nothing I hate more than a rat, he said.

He knew he couldn't stop himself now. He felt suddenly light, like he was being pulled out of himself somehow. A tingle behind the eyes, pins and needles all across the chest. The butcher's hands did nothing to stop the low swooping arc of the knife as it uppercut into his big belly, three four five times.

You mouthy fuck, said Bats, and as the butcher groaned sickly, he gave him one last thrust, downward into the gob.

The butcher fell backwards onto his hunkers before keeling over onto his side, the light coating of sawdust soaking up blood once again.

It was only then, seeing him lifeless and grotesque on the shop floor that Bats came to. Panic flashed cold all over him, and dropping the knife, he ran out the door, past his car and into the wet night.

In the woods now, in the still pissing rain, he thumbed the broken skin on his knuckles. Broken from where they grazed the butcher's teeth. Mouthy cunt, he mumbled to himself.

Under the canopy of trees, the rain changed to sporadic drops and in the distance a light mist backlit by the breaking sun. It had taken all night, but the Inspector had finally gotten the young Door lad to talk. The woods, he had said. The woods.

In their wet gear and lead by the Inspector, the guards spread out in a dragnet combing the woods from east to west. One of the guards pointed out the squeal of a buzzard flying high overhead. Beautiful creatures, he said.

They found Bats Collins soaked to the skin, teeth chattering and curled up into a ball in a child's makeshift hut. A few twigs charred at the ends signalled a weak effort to get a fire going. When the Inspector's shadow crossed his face, Bats opened his pale bleary eyes to regard him. He made a stiff effort to sit up, his bloodied hands coming slowly out of the warmth of his armpits.

It was all fun and games, wasn't it, Collins? said the Inspector.

Bats shivered a meek defence. He said it wasn't him.

Wasn't you that what?

That did it, he said.

Did what now?

The guards had all gathered round the camp and were looking down at Bats with one big grin among them.

Bats' face crumpled into anguished sobs and he lay back with his arm over his eyes. The Inspector told the guards to lift him up and get him to the station and as he watched the men take Bats away he shook his head, and wondered what God-forsaken place they had sent him to.

For the murder of the butcher, Malachy Mahon, Barry 'Bats' Collins was given life in prison. When asked why he did it – why claim all those natural deaths – he said he thought the town needed a bit of livening up. He said that as much as he'll be condemned for his actions, they'll be talking about him for years. He said that, at the end of the day, what he did was entertainment. It was a public service. When asked had he no remorse for killing the butcher, he said he had, of course.

I just saw red, Judge, he said. You know yourself what that's like.

For the spread of misinformation and wasting the precious time of An Garda Siochana, young Ollie Door was fined 500 euro and given a slap on the wrist. He was talked about for a while, avoided in the street and in the pubs, but in the end his part was put down to him being harmless and easily lead. He was innocent in a naïve sort of way. It was never revealed that Paul Óg was an informant and since Bats, the real menace, was gone, the town went back to normal. Or at least it tried to. For months after, the Inspector was visited by local people eager to give eye-witness testimony on all those killings.

But they weren't killings, he tried to tell Deirdre Rourke.

But I saw them outside Eileen's house the night she died. Two little gougers in hoodies, smoking fags.

That might be true, Ms Rourke. You may have seen that, but Mrs Murtagh died of a brain aneurysm.

Aye, she said. But I wouldn't put it past those two to have caused it.

Even Big John Breslin tried to claim that the two lads had killed his brother Martin. He said they were up and down the road outside his house at all hours for weeks. They drove Martin mad with their footsteps, Inspector.

The Inspector let out a sigh, deflated. The string of faces sitting opposite changed with the turn of each day, with the constant flow of time. They came sniffling into sodden tissues; they came in confidence; they came without end, telling tales, claiming to have seen, eager to be a part of the narrative. And no matter how many times they were told it had all been a hoax, they were determined to go on believing that Bats Collins was Ireland's first serial killer. What sort of place had they sent him to altogether?

Balkan Syndrome

by Yanita Georgieva

We are plagued by an endless summer. There are crueller afflictions.

We are low on pennies but lax with the pennies we have.

There will always be dinner for ten, always sand in our shoes,

always a medicine advert stuck in our heads. *Annie is happy*

because she does not have cystitis. In every juniper garden

there is a woman pulling threads out of the spines

of green beans, crippling them gently. Red peppers oozing

out of their skins. It's easy, this plague. You can bathe in the coral

blues. Wink at the hills. Pick up any hot-bellied seashell

and press it flat to your ear. It is ready to tell you a story —

if you're lucky, a secret. *You'll never believe what I saw here,*

is how it always begins. You will never hear how it ends.

Twilight Interval

Translated by Everly Lovefield

Beneath your hair, your eyes are like
Fistfuls of light through spider webs.

Your summer smile, dyed by the dawn,
Is the same as Sarah's arrogant smile.

My gaze is hypnotized by that wild ringlet
Where divine sapphire weds ruby.

Your Indian perfumes, your salves and scarves
Astound the simple artlessness of water lilies.

Hatred of love and love of hatred
Share my heart and uncertain soul.

With a pale forefinger, benevolent Death points
At the lunar hill where the flint lightens.

In the distance an arpeggio deteriorates and exalts.
I want to purify my soul in the snow…

Behold, more beautiful than childish Adonis,
The death of Adonia in a shroud of lilies.

Intervalle crépusculaire

by Renée Vivien

Tes yeux sous tes cheveux sont comme des poignées
De rayons à travers des toiles d'araignées.

Ton sourire d'été, que l'aube colora,
Est pareil au sourire orgueilleux de Sara.

Mon regard s'hypnotise à cette fauve boucle
Où le divin saphir épouse l'escarboucle.

Tes parfums indiens, tes onguents et tes fards
Etonnent la candeur simple des nénuphars.

La haine de l'amour et l'amour de la haine
Se partagent mon cœur et mon âme incertaine.

La bienfaisante Mort montre d'un pâle index
La colline lunaire où blondit le silex.

Au lointain s'exaspère et s'exalte un arpège.
Je veux purifier mon âme dans la neige…

Vois, plus belle que le puéril Adonis,
Mourir Adonéa dans un linceul de lys.

Note on the Author

by Everly Lovefield

Despite Renée Vivien's literary accomplishments, her work is not well known in English-speaking spheres, and English translations of her writing are few and far between. Vivien (1877–1909) was a British poet, writer, and translator who lived in Paris for most of her life and wrote in French. Her largely autobiographical works reflect the values of both the Symbolist and Parnassian literary movements. During her lifetime, she wrote twelve collections of poetry in verse, seven collections of poetry in prose, twelve novels, and much more. She is most renowned for being Sappho's first lesbian translator, and she is also considered one of the first openly lesbian writers.

As a lesbian and neopagan with feminist views, Vivien lived during a time in which aspects of her identity were persecuted and deemed unacceptable by wider society. Nevertheless, she loved and worshipped who she wanted, wrote what she liked and lived authentically. Both her life and her writing subverted societal expectations, as can be seen in 'Twilight Interval'. The narrative act of transforming Adonis into 'Adonia' not only boldly reimagines a women-centred mythology, but also serves as a triumphant expression of Sapphic love. Given Vivien's sexuality, her writing is particularly important in the context of the queer literary canon and queer history. All in all, her work deserves recognition from a wider audience.

When I stumbled upon Vivien's poetry, it was love at first read. I felt connected to her despite our displacement in time and space. Besides Vivien's way with words and imagery, a translator translating another translator's work felt significant to me and further deepened my sense of affinity for her. And deep down, perhaps I wish I had written Vivien's poems myself. Even if I'm not capable of her writing feats, at least my translation can act as a bridge between her and the English-speaking world.

Evidently, translating Vivien's poetry posed challenges, especially since she writes in a technically precise way using fixed rhyme schemes and meter. At first, I endeavoured to preserve the rhyme schemes, but the result was stilted and did not faithfully convey her voice or style. For that reason, I altered my approach and relied on different poetic methods, or 'tools' as Yves Bonnefoy calls them, to create rhythm and sonority in my translation. To compensate for the lack of rhyming, my principal strategies were assonance and consonance in 'Twilight Interval'. For me, translating Vivien's poetry was a lesson in not unnecessarily chaining oneself to the source text's formal features if other 'tools' are more beneficial to the translation and truer to the original.

The Marksman

by Rory Say

The phone that hung on the hallway wall rang in bursts of six. In my head I kept a careful tally. As soon as Da's voice on the machine finished its recorded message, encouraging the caller to state their name and number, the ringing would return, louder, it always seemed, than the times before. Under no circumstances was I to answer the phone while by myself in the house.

I disliked being left alone. It was hard not to imagine the house as in some way aware of me, able to read my thoughts and detect my movements. With this in mind, I had been lying motionless on top of my bedcovers, looking down the lighted hall, when the phone first startled me.

Earlier, I'd had to get up and turn all the lights back on after Mammy had left the place in darkness on her way to eight o'clock Mass at nine, more than an hour after Da had gone to what he called work. She must take me for stupid. I'd heard her at the cupboards in the kitchen and could see from my room the way she struggled with her boots and her coat, a shoulder to the wall. These signs were known to me. I could read them as surely as I could read the hands of a clock.

How long a minute lasted when you watched it elapse. It was the clock on my side table I was watching when the ringing finally cut out and the house fell silent. After eleven. In the renewed quiet I heard once again the watery sounds of hunger in my stomach—harder now to ignore—and I thought of the biscuits and milk I'd seen Da put in the fridge that afternoon. I spent a long while trying to ease my mind so that I could move, but before I had it settled a car braked loudly out front. I listened to a door open, followed by the clapping of a woman's shoes on the footpath to the house.

'Gillian!' a hushed voice called. There was a pause before a hand rattled the front door's handle while another beat at the frame. 'Gilly, for the love of God, open up if you're in there.'

It was then that I recognized the voice of my auntie Maureen. Quietly, I slid from bed and crept down the hall, still cautious of the noise I made but grateful that my time alone had reached its end. I opened the door as it was still being struck.

'What's going on here?' Auntie Maureen said, her eyes searching me up and down.

I glanced over my shoulder at the empty hall.

'You're not left here alone, are you? Look at me, Kate.'

But the best I could do was look at her shoes.

'Where's your mother?'

'Da went out.'

I could feel the heat of her gaze on my face. 'Have you heard anything, Kate? Has anyone been round?'

I shook my head no.

'Where's your mother.'

For a moment I searched for something safe to say. Though I hated when Mammy left me alone at night, I didn't want the lie she'd told to cause any trouble.

'Katy?'

'She went up to Mass.'

A sharp sigh left my auntie's mouth. 'Jesus wept,' she said, and crossed herself. 'That sister of mine. Devil the Mass she brings herself to.'

I backed away to let her inside. She kept her coat on and told me to go and sit in my room with the door closed till she'd made a call or two out in the hall.

So maybe it was Auntie Maureen who'd rung the house over and over while I lay in bed, listening and counting while Da's voice on the machine said the same thing in the same way again and again. But then why after trying so many times hadn't she left a message?

A knock came to the door as I was turning all this over. It opened a crack and my auntie's head appeared.

'You've heard nothing at all?' she said.

Again, I shook my head. 'Heard what? What's happened, Auntie Maureen?'

'Go and get some things ready,' she said. 'You'll be coming along with me.'

My cousin Tom stood out front when we arrived at my auntie and uncle's, clutching himself with his long arms and shivering in his pyjamas. On his face was a giddy look that told me he knew something he wasn't meant to. I never liked to be near him.

'What in God's name are you doing out in your jammies, Thomas MacIntyre?' Auntie Maureen shouted from her rolled-down window. 'Get back inside, you.'

Tom hugged himself tighter and, giggling like a boy half his age, disappeared through the open door behind him. There had been no words spoken on the short drive here.

Inside the house, Uncle John stood in the centre of the kitchen, his attention focused on the bare wall above the stove.

'Hi'ya, Uncle John,' I called as I came in.

He turned his head toward me, his thick features immobile. 'Is that you, Kate?'

'Didn't I tell you on the phone?' Auntie Maureen brushed by on her way to her husband. 'Left on her own with no one come round to see her. The shame of it.'

A tug came to my sleeve. Tom had emerged from the sitting room and was smiling at me, his tongue in the hole between two top teeth.

'You're to be in my room,' he said. 'C'mere till I show you.'

I knew very well where Tom's room was, but all the same I let him lead me by the wrist through the kitchen, past his whispering parents, to the narrow hall at the back of the house. He went in ahead and flicked the light.

'And where'll you be?' I asked, standing in the doorway where he'd dropped my arm.

'Just in the sittin' room.'

'I can go there.'

'Da says no. G'wan.' With a flop of his arm he indicated the unmade bed, on which socks and a white t-shirt lay entangled in the sheets.

I placed the bag I'd brought with me upright in a clearing of clothes. Tom asked what was in it and I answered him vaguely. I expected that he might tidy the bed, but he only stood by the window and watched as I crouched to my bag and pretended to search for something.

'I wonder does this make us brother and sister?' he said.

A feeling like cold water slid down my spine. I turned to ask him what he meant and found my auntie's face in the doorway, a cigarette jutting from her lips.

'Are you hungry, wee pet?' she said to me. 'Could I fix anything?'

I shook my head no. 'I'm fine, Auntie.'

The truth was that I wanted very badly to eat, but more than that I wanted to be left alone, or to at least be away from Tom. I tried to think of some way to explain that I'd much rather sleep in the sitting room than in the bed I'd been offered.

'Won't I make yous both some hot cocoa,' said Auntie Maureen, lighting her cigarette and jetting blue smoke towards us.

I followed her back to the kitchen, where I sat at the square table against the wall and watched Uncle John drink whiskey from a small glass. He seemed hesitant to acknowledge me. Tom came in a minute later and put his back to the counter, the same smirk on his face he'd had when I arrived. I could almost hear the question before he asked it.

'Can we tell her yet?'

There was a loud bang of glass on the table as my uncle and auntie both shouted his name. He began to laugh in a frightened sort of way until Uncle John got up in a flash and hit the side of his head with a hard open hand, sending him squealing to the sitting room. It was quiet after that.

I brought the cup of cocoa and plate of crackers back to Tom's room and closed the door. Sitting on the edge of the mattress, I ate the dry crackers one after the other and only felt hungrier once I'd finished, like all they'd done was dig a deeper pit inside of me. The cocoa burnt my mouth when I tried to drink it.

A knock came and the door opened.

'You're all right, pet?' Auntie Maureen asked as she entered the room.

'Fine, Auntie.'

The phone rang in the kitchen and my uncle answered it at once, his low voice inaudible. I no longer had any idea what time it was. It felt like I had been here for much longer than I knew I had been, like it was a different night altogether to the one I'd spent lying awake on my bed, too frightened to move, even to undress.

'Aren't you a good wee girl,' my auntie said. She picked the clothes off Tom's bed and tossed them in a corner, then produced a fresh cigarette from the pocket of her blouse.

'I suppose you'd like to know,' she said in a soft, regretful voice, leaning carefully against the door at her back, 'that your poor father's up now with God in heaven.'

She allowed a moment for this information to settle. It sounded too absurd to take seriously. I never thought you could die unless it said so on the telly or in the paper, or unless you were very old and everyone you knew had had time to come and sit with you and tell you things they remembered.

'Did you hear me, Kate?' said my auntie. She put a flame to the tip of her cigarette and deeply inhaled.

'Was it a bomb?' I asked. 'Did the men blow him up in the car?'

For a while there was quiet. I wasn't sure whether my auntie was considering the question or pretending it hadn't been asked. A memory came from the summer before last when me and Da had both run screaming back from the tide at Narin Strand in Donegal, and afterward he'd bought me a ninety-nine on our way to the caravan even though we both knew Mammy had dinner waiting. *That right there's between you and me*, he'd said to my ear, a secret. They called him a hard man, my Da, but he was never that to me. Not once.

'You'd not want to know such a thing,' Auntie Maureen said at last, smoking thoughtfully. 'You shouldn't ask what you'd not want to know.'

I thought about this, about what I wanted to know.

'Where's Ma?' I asked.

Another pause. 'Your mother will be just grand,' said my auntie. She stepped out into the hall but kept her head in the room. 'I'm very sorry, Kate. We all are. Your daddy loved you very much and he's up now with God in heaven. Do you know that?'

I'd never been able to visualise the place she mentioned, though it had been described to me many times at school. And what would Da do there? It didn't make sense that I wouldn't see him in the morning, that I wouldn't be able to crawl into his bed while he slept and hug his warmth without waking him.

'Now you get some sleep, wee pet,' said Auntie Maureen, beginning to close the door. 'Sure isn't the wake in the afternoon tomorrow.'

I did my best to ignore the spectacle of Tom at breakfast, eating boiled eggs on burnt toast with rashers the colour of a tongue. He liked to eat with his greasy hands and suck clean his fingers, a slapping sound like a cow as he chewed. It helped that I was half starved and could hardly think.

After we'd finished and our plates had been piled with the pans in the sink, Auntie Maureen and Uncle John put on their coats and hurried out the door, mentioning arrangements. I tried to follow them outside and was told to stay where I was. Everything's grand. Tom would look after me.

Tom was only half a year older but liked to pretend we were worlds apart, which I suppose we were. There was nothing about him that didn't disgust me.

'I wonder does this make us brother and sister?' he said when we were alone, repeating himself with an idiot grin.

'I don't think so,' I said uncertainly, and sank down again at the table. Tom stood a foot away, eyeing me like I might try to escape. 'We're cousins because our mammies are sisters,' I explained. 'Our daddies aren't related. We have different last names.'

Tom's face went slack as he digested this, his tongue pressed to the white worm of snot escaping from a nostril. 'But now you don't have a daddy,' he said, having puzzled it out. 'My daddy could be your new daddy and then we'd be brother and sister.'

It was too awful to consider, let alone discuss.

'I think I'd like to go outside.' I held the table as I got to my feet, all the blood in my legs having gone somewhere else. 'You don't have to come,' I said to Tom, who'd turned to follow.

'I want to,' he said, and pushed past me on his way to his shoes. 'Daddy got me a gun I have out back. C'mere till I show you.'

We stepped out into cold sunlight that stung the eyes. I didn't really want to be outside, I realised, but neither could I think of any place else I wanted to be. I wondered why Mammy hadn't come round by now. Maybe she was dead, too.

'Just back here,' Tom said, pulling me by the arm down the side of the house.

We came to a small square of balding grass in the back, at the far end of which a dozen or so dented beer cans stood crookedly on top of two cinder blocks. Tom ran off to a tool shed and returned holding a gun.

'Is it real?' I asked, looking warily at the miniature rifle Tom held out for my appraisal.

'It isn't a toy,' he said proudly, 'but it mightn't kill you. It shoots these, so it does.'

He took from his pocket three tiny white balls, which he allowed me to hold and inspect. They weighed nothing but felt bone-hard when I squeezed them in turn.

'Watch,' said Tom, snatching them from my hand and thumbing one into a slot at the top of his rifle. He raised the gun's butt to his shoulder, took careful aim, and fired with a cork-stopper *pop*. In the same instant a yellow can of Magners went spinning to the ground with a tinny click.

'*Dead!*' Tom shouted, raising his rifle in triumph. '*Dead, dead—shot to the head!*'

The memory came, as it did now and then in moments of uncertain fear, of the time a few years back when my search for Christmas presents had brought me to the blankets and old clothes stuffed beneath Mammy and Daddy's bed. Instead of wrapped gifts I discovered a wooden case containing two handguns, a belt of ammunition, and a dismantled rifle not unlike the one Tom now waved above his head. It was one of those memories that becomes less real the more often you bring it to mind, so that now I can hardly be sure it happened, even though I know it did. I'd gone back to look again.

'Go and sit over there,' Tom said, pointing to the cinder blocks.

I looked at him. 'Why would I do a thing like that?'

'Ye needn't be scared.' He plugged another white ball into the rifle. 'I won't hit you. I'm a right marksman, so I am.'

He pointed now with the gun's barrel at the spot he'd have me sit. I hesitated for as long as I could, and then, seeing no alternative, moved slowly across the grass to the cinder blocks, where I set aside a few cans and sat down.

'Hold one to your head,' said Tom.

My back straightened. 'I don't want to,' I told him. 'You might shoot my eye out.'

'I won't,' Tom insisted. 'Ye needn't be scared. G'wan.'

He motioned with his gun as he spoke. Already it seemed like another memory out of place. Would I feel more frightened when I thought back to this? Would Tom shoot me if I stood up and tried to leave?

'G'wan,' said Tom, lifting his rifle.

I felt with my hand for the nearest can and raised it to the top of my head, resting it on my hair.

'Can I cover my eyes?' I asked.

'No,' said Tom, 'but you can close them if you like.'

Holding myself as still as I could, I closed my eyes and opened them again after nothing had happened. Tom stood across the grass, statue-still, aiming intently at what looked like my face. I suddenly felt the imagined impact as a sharp itch inside my eye, and I put my free hand to my face as the gun went off.

'*You moved!*' Tom howled. It took a second to realise that this meant I had been spared. I blinked and brought my fingers to my eyes behind their lids, relishing sight and the lack of agony. 'I would've hit it if you didn't *move!*'

The can I'd forgotten fell from my head as I rose from the block. Tom, fumbling with his rifle, shouted at me to pick it up and stay still, just where I was.

'I'll be right back,' I said, heading back the way we'd come. 'I'm just off to use the toilet.'

Tom followed me with an empty look till I made it round the side of the house, where I stopped to catch my breath, almost laughing with relief. Behind me, I heard the hollow *pop* from the gun, the metallic kiss of a can sent flying, and I bolted for the front door.

'Dead, dead—shot to the head! Dead, dead—shot to the head!'

The hot bath ripened my skin to a soft pink. My fingers withered. I stayed in too long in the hope I'd be forgotten about and left behind, but now my auntie called through the locked door while rattling its handle—the wake was at three, and she needed the bathroom so she could put on her face.

'Have you nothing black to wear?' she said when I let her in.

I looked down at my green sweater and grey skirt. 'I have some black at home,' I said.

She considered this. 'It'll be all right,' she said. 'Tom'll lend you a shirt.'

In the back of the car Tom got up on his knees to see his head reflected in the rear-view. His hair had been combed and parted, hardened stiff by a clear gel I'd seen my auntie mix with saliva from her tongue. He looked like someone else who looked something like himself, and he began to laugh before my uncle snapped.

'Why's it called a wake?' Tom asked while we idled at a light, and he was told to sit back down and stop fussing with his hair.

It was clear that I had no role to play when we arrived at my granny's. The adults spoke quietly in smoky clusters, everyone drinking from glasses of stout, whiskey, or wine. Bottles stood open on every surface, and from somewhere a woman's voice sang a slow song. I wondered about Mammy. Auntie Maureen had told me that she hadn't taken the news well and likely wouldn't make it to the wake, but she'd be just grand in the end. I wondered why nobody had asked how I had taken the news, because I didn't want to go to the wake either.

And yet here I was, the air in the kitchen turning white with smoke. I took a glass from the counter and filled it with tap water, sipping now and then as I watched my aunts, uncles, and cousins enter and leave the room down the hall, crossing themselves before and after, wiping at their eyes and noses. Sometimes someone approached to touch my hair and tell me they were sorry, but more often they only reached for a bottle at my back, or an ashtray. Maybe I could even leave without being seen, I thought, or without seeing Da. I began to envision my escape when Tom found me.

'Have you seen him yet?' he asked, excited, his mouth filled with cheese and pickle.

I shook my head no. 'Not yet,' I said. 'I'm not sure I will.'

Water spilled from my glass as Tom grabbed the sleeve of his own borrowed shirt. I told him to let go but he held on tight, pretending not to hear. Adults in black stepped aside and raised their drinks higher — *sorry, sorry, excuse me, sorry.*

There was no one else in the room when we entered. The guest bed had been taken out, the chairs pushed to the wall, the mirror taken down. There was nothing but a long wooden box with a man lying inside it, a mounted cross above the head. Tom let go of me but I didn't leave. *Say goodbye to him,* my auntie had said that morning, and then again in the car. *Tell him how you loved him.*

But I hardly recognized the man that lay in the box, and my mouth stayed shut. I looked down at the dark suit I'd never seen, at the crossed arms holding a rifle to the breast. I looked at the lips, sealed in a downward curve, and at the heavy clumps of makeup concealing bruises on the forehead. The fine yellow hair was combed straight back as it never was in life, and it was all I could do not to reach out with my hands and try to fix it.

Pomegranate

by Gráinne Ní Nualláin

It starts with a trickle. Just a thorn prick, ivory bleeding crimson. Just a flicker, then silence.

The roar comes unannounced in the night; it begins as an avalanche does, a single stone shifting in the shadows. Then every particle, every ounce of hope, nothing left unturned, just a daylight daydream, fleeing in the dark:

I cannot breathe for you.

A snowflake on the window melts away.

And this is the first time. And this is me screaming for a thing I've never known. Footsteps on the hardwood, a tiny buttercup chin, but no cry from the bedroom, no call from sleepless nights, just a wasteland of bodies lining the hall, all the things I couldn't carry.

Losing count of doctor's offices, shining pristine walls, stethoscopes and speculums. I lie open on the table, a cadaver with a pulse. They say nothing is wrong. I burn. They say the scans are clear. I ache. I tell them it's slowly devouring my organs, one by one: lungs, colon, heart. Psychosomatic: codeword for hysteria. A wolf in sheep's clothing, and Freud applauds in the beyond. The doctor writes a prescription for an increase in sertraline, a new pill.

Azealia

Yasmin

Cilest

Ovranette

Dianette

Why do they name them like goddesses, like flowers, like beautiful girls running through lavender fields?

The doctor promises the coil will resolve everything. There is no anaesthetic when they tear me open. Labour, but no cry, no sign that you will ever wake.

Persephone dreams of me, pomegranate seeds in tight palms, turning water to wine on her fingertips.

I wake. I bleed. I break.

Still, I hope. Still, I wonder if you'll grow —

despite the odds.

Sometimes, I sing you sweet lullabies and wonder if you hear me. Sunburst daisy, blooming daylight. Sometimes, I wonder if you'll ever be mine: all arms and shoulders, tiny petal hands, the softest of velvets, bringing you to life.

Dawn breaks, and the chorus is a funeral march. All I have ever known is the dream of you. I yearn for the smell of your skin, warm and bright and breathing, in my arms. I whisper to the morning sky:

Tell me how the earth-

scattered tulips,

red stains

on a quiet bed,

teaches us humility,

teaches us forgiveness?

Tell me there's an end

To this silence.

Every ripple, a new wave of shame. Every crimson drop, a reminder, a failure to us both. What I lack is. What I lack is. If I say it out loud does it make it true?

I refuse.

I'm not superstitious but —

I smother myself in rose quartz and down bottles of cough syrup. I press my knees to my chest, prop pillows to elevate my legs. I buy a caul from the local herbalist, press it to my skin, protect it like a child. If this is the closest I ever come, I will love you wholly, unashamedly, always. I will never regret the trying.

I cannot shake the feeling I was born for this. I cannot shake the feeling I'm *too late.*

Our language drips

by Simon Maddrell

in the dark   I am afraid   of meeting

my emptiness   but I must

return   to the isle of my birth

before I become   my own extinction.

Our native *Yn Gaelg*

was nearly silenced

from what   only it   can express.

I nearly zipped   my own lips

in a black-bagged lack   of understanding

that it is language   that restores our place,

that speaks   louder than any plinth,

that   when it cries   deepens the sea.

It is near impossible   to describe   the sun

rising   but it is possible   to feel

the language   of the sun   setting

on darkness.

Yn Gaelg: Manx Gaelic

Art Class

by E.E. King

Photographed by Eric Wallengren

The Roommate

by Karla Hirsch

The body appears on a Sunday and it appears in your bathtub. It's a woman, somewhere between your own age and *really old*. She's thin, bones protruding, elbows sticking out of her short-sleeved blouse inquisitively, collar bone curved like the side of a violin.

You've heard of this phenomenon. The government's attempts at removing the bodies have been fruitless. They reappear until left where they've decided to rest and eventually dissolve without a trace. From all you've heard, it's not necessarily unpleasant to house a body for a while. They don't smell. They make no sounds. Still, you're annoyed. The bathtub? It's inconvenient. You order an *expiration consultant*.

How long will it take? you ask the bulky man in your bathroom. He inspects your tub with a concentrated frown, lips pursed.

Hard to say, he says and lifts her right arm, holding the fragile wrist carefully. His hand is covered with wiry black hairs. Even his knuckles wear small shrubs.

Nothing we can do but wait, he shrugs.

When he's gone, you return to the bathroom and look at the woman. She seems content in her porcelain bed. Pale skin, old-fashioned tweed skirt. You imagine she worked in a library. They've become redundant these days, but some nostalgics still cling to them and regularly drum up petitions to keep them open.

Your new situation becomes a nuisance when you need to wash your hair the next morning.

This is less than ideal, you mumble and bend over the sink, scooping handfuls of tepid water over your head. You throw the body an annoyed look. It's unimpressed.

When you leave work that night, you walk through empty streets. Few people use offices now. They stay at home to work remotely then stay at home to play online or meet friends in chatrooms. In front of your building, you are greeted by two racoons busily raiding the trash under a flickering streetlamp. They ignore you. The apartment tower looms over you in the darkness, stuffed with strangers, the black and white windows a disarranged chessboard. Inside, people live like pralines in a box — each wrapped in their little compartment, separated by walls and differences.

You go straight to the bathroom and check on the body.

Hello, you say quietly.

When you go to bed that night, you keep the bathroom door open. It feels almost as if someone's only sleeping next door.

On day two, you drink your morning coffee in the bathroom. It seems rude not to. On day three, you bring back Chinese takeaway — your weekly Wednesday treat. You drag one of your red folding chairs from the kitchen into the bathroom and set the food down on the bathtub's rim. Although the body's eyes are closed, it feels as if they're following your movements. You watch a football game together. Because you like to clean a little before you go to bed, you keep the bathroom door open and while you dust your two slim bookshelves and the generic metal couch table that comes with flats now, you tell her about your day — about your intrusive boss who looks you up and down whenever he talks to you, about your colleague who pretends you don't exist. The body listens patiently.

You get used to washing your hair over the sink. When you pass restaurants, you imagine what she might have liked to eat and buy it. You try sushi for the first time. Outside your building, the racoons still ignore you, but the way to the door seems shorter.

She might have liked music you decide one night. When you ask her, her face is as stoic as ever, but you've learnt to ignore her rigidness. You ask your *Techmate* to play something nice. The system takes a few seconds to load as if surprised by this unusual request, but then plays a Leonard Cohen song. A choir fills the room, and a low, melancholy voice rises — low, melancholy words that come to you like arms around your waist, like hands that lift your hands, and you sway with them like strands of reed by the river, overcome by a warm wind or a storm, dancing to the end of love.

You know that she's gone before you turn around. Outside your hollow room, the stubborn night expands, the wind moans the woods to sleep, and you think of the racoons that you cannot see, only sense, beyond the unyielding walls of your house.

Road Trip

by Malinda Meadows

In this time span of your absence
every cell in my body has turned anew,
and I realize they don't know you either.

So I propose, in true Americana fashion,
we plot a course   and make up for lost time.

Heading west on I-70 from Ohio, I'll start by telling you
        how the threads that once tethered me
                were spun only of sugar,

        and collected on the windowsill like snow.

You'll be annoyed when you learn
our wedding was just an intimate dinner,
and there was no priest or spire in sight,
but you'll laugh at how my husband
passed around potatoes to our guests.

That last part will take longer to explain,
but thankfully Kansas is flat

                and its sky expansive,
                    so that it leaves plenty of room for words.

Somewhere near the state border,
I'll humour you by playing ABBA, rolling my eyes as I pretend
I haven't spent years memorizing your favourite.

You'll wonder about grandchildren,
But only ask this while I'm busy concentrating

on the winding
        mountain roads
                through Colorado,

                                          I'll stop short of making a joke

                          because what humour can be found
                                      in broken glass
                                  and twisted metal.

I'll also tell you how I think that every time
the sun
        dips
                and Utah gets dark,

                        it creates a whole different shade of night
                        that hints at the very madness of living.

We'll keep driving until we reach the Pacific,
the farthest west you've ever been.

Then we'll draw a line
straight
down
the 5
and head south toward my new home,

stopping once more at my spot near the cliff.
And all my mind will see is the water breaking the reflected moon
into a rogue wave of headlights,

        cutting
                blinding
                      slamming you off course,

                          when you were only
                            miles from
                              safety.

And when you ask me if it still hurts,

I'll say it has softened like sea glass,

but is everywhere I go.

And before I can ask you what it's like to be gone from this Earth,

                        I'm all alone again,
                driving the final stretch toward home.

An Interview with Danny Denton

Danny Denton's biggest influences, he tells me, are writers who 'make anything feel possible', whether it's the unorthodox beauty of Anne Carson's sentences, the twisted surrealism of David Lynch, or Denis Johnson's narrator, Fuckhead, suddenly breaking away from a short story to berate the reader. 'That's the stuff I love the most,' Danny says.

This feeling of possibility is something he has successfully managed to distill into his own work. Both of his novels to date — *The Earlie King & the Kid in Yellow* (2018) and *All Along the Echo* (2022) — interweave the lives of their characters through an ambitious blend of narrative styles. Chapters take the form of everything from play scenes to radio transcripts, and the tone can shift from despair to hilarity and back again in the course of a single paragraph.

Danny's latest novel, *All Along The Echo*, tells the stories of local radio chatshow host, Tony, and those who call into his show. Following its publication, I sat down with Danny in his office in UCC, where he lectures in Creative Writing, to discuss his writing life and his relationship to the written word from a young age.

Stephen Brophy: What is the first book you remember reading and/or the latest book you've read?

Danny Denton: I was left off in the library when I was six or seven and I picked a book off the wrong shelf without the librarian noticing. It was an apocalyptic children's book that was way too old for me where this boy wakes up and his dog is dead. He looks in the next bedroom and his brother is dead, in the next bedroom after that his parents are dead. And I just started balling crying. My mam threw the book in the fire and had to pay the librarian a fiver for it the next week.

The first book I remember reading in one sitting was Fantastic Mr. Fox. I think I was nine. I stayed up all night reading it.

SB: What type of writing other than fiction would you like to attempt that you haven't tried yet?

DD: When I did my MA in writing I learned loads from it, but the main thing I learned is that I'm an absolutely useless poet. So not poetry.

I've seen five or six things in the theatre in my life that I thought were absolutely amazing, but I wouldn't have seen enough of it to write.

SB: And if you had the interest in it you maybe got it out of your system in the play scenes in *The Earlie King & the Kid in Yellow*?

DD: Maybe. I love reading plays, actually. I wouldn't mind trying to write for TV. I think that would be an interesting thing to try. I had this idea about something that could be set where I live in Passage West where all these things were happening that wouldn't work in a novel but that I could definitely write a TV show of. I got quite enthusiastic about that for a couple of months, but when push came to shove I didn't have that much time to write and if I only have three hours a day to write I'm going to use them to write fiction. But I definitely wouldn't rule out television.

SB: Which writers have influenced you most and was there a process of writing them out of your system before your own voice showed up on the page?

DD: Early days, I was definitely over-influenced. I wrote a novel that never got published that was me trying to be some mixture of John McGahern and Dermot Healy.

So you could argue that that novel was me writing them out of my system or writing enough like someone else that I thought, no I want to do it my own way.

Hemingway was a big one and I think that's probably a young man thing. Young men read Hemingway and they want to be him.

SB: In terms of the sentences?

DD: Yeah, they try to write these sentences that are very standoffish and very straightforward. I probably wrote a lot of bad Hemingway sentence rip-offs around then, although then I was mostly writing in a journal and not trying to write fiction. This is before I was ever trying to get published. I do have a specific memory of when I started writing like myself, and probably stopped apeing other styles so much. It was 2014. I was commissioned to write non-fiction for the London issue of *The Stinging Fly*. Declan [Meade] gave me a 3,000 word limit. And I came back to him with an 11,000 word piece of stream of consciousness modernist fiction. I was like, 'I'm very sorry.' But, fair play to them, they published it. That was the first time I felt like I was doing it completely the way I wanted to do it. And I feel like everything I've done since has been kind of in that style. Or in my style at least.

Of course I am still happy to be influenced and pushed by other writers. Samuel Beckett is an influence. Roberto Bolaño. I would love to be as free as he is on the page. Anne Carson liberates me. I always try and read her every six months or so, because it just blows wide open what's possible. And I think that was a big thing for me. Blowing open what's possible to do what *must* be done.

SB: Do you ever find your work influenced by artists from other media such as music or cinema?

DD: I would love to write a book the way David Lynch writes a movie. I absolutely love the way Anne Carson writes poetry, the way Stephen Sexton writes poetry. I think the thing they all have in common is that anything feels possible. I love that kind of stuff.

SB: Well that's definitely in your books. They can take any kind of a turn. You can have a character who's having an existential crisis and goes to hide from the world in a public toilet to gather themselves and all of a sudden the stranger in the next cubicle is hearing their confession.

DD: Yeah. One of the things you ask yourself when you're writing is, 'can I get away with this?' And if I was overly influenced by realist fiction I would probably feel it's not possible to do something like that. But because I've seen Twin Peaks a few times anything can happen. Nothing is as it seems. I mean that not only in terms of narrative or plot. I mean it in terms of sentence as well. Stephen Sexton and Anne Carson can write sentences that don't seem possible until you read them. I don't think I've ever written a sentence like that yet. The aim is to hopefully get there at some point.

SB: Have you ever had a writing mentor? If not, who would you choose as a dream mentor?

DD: I've had several mentors over the years. Mike McCormack was a great mentor to me during my Masters in Creative Writing in Galway. He was very supportive and great with advice. Also, when you work with editors, they become your mentors. As I said, Declan Meade at *The Stinging Fly* edited my first published story and I learned loads from him. Tom Morris edited another early story of mine with a very light touch. Sometimes a mentor's job is to give you confidence, to let you know you're on the right path. It's not always to say, 'that's not how you use a comma'.

My two book editors, Max Porter at Granta, and James Roxburgh at Atlantic were amazing. They were both great on the line. They'll show you how sentences can improve or how ideas can be seen through without telling you what to do. A good mentor or editor, they just put the work first. It's not all about making the sentences better, either. Sometimes it's 'What is the person trying to do? What is the project and how can I help them achieve the project?' And all my mentors had that in common.

SB: If you're struggling with a project and you feel a new idea calling you do you chase the new idea or do you believe in forcing yourself to finish everything you start?

DD: I don't finish everything I start. I can develop fake enthusiasm for a piece, but if it's really not working, then good luck to it. But I never delete anything. Everything is kept on a file on a computer.

SB: So are there leftovers from projects that morph into something else?

DD: There's a whole 30,000 word narrative strand cut out of *The Earlie King & the Kid in Yellow*. Max [Porter] said look, this really bogs everything else down, but it's up to you whether you want to keep it or not. And sure enough, when I took it out I had to make some significant changes, but it made it a way better book. So I still have those 30,000 words about a data terrorist. I often wondered whether it would make a novella, but at the moment it's not an idea that I want to chase. I've kind of moved on from it.

SB: The dialogue, particularly in *All Along The Echo*, rings so true to me as a Cork person that I wondered, do you take notes of overheard dialogue, thinking, 'I'll use that some day' and also is it something that's refined by reading drafts of your work out loud to yourself?

DD: I always give the advice to read your work out loud. You can hear things when it's read aloud that just don't get exposed on a page or a screen. It can be embarrassing or whatever, particularly if you're house-sharing and people think you're up there talking to yourself, but it's crucial, I think, in progressing the sentences.

DD: There's a particular line of dialogue that I heard once. I was walking past a table and heard a woman say, 'like, I was in a WhatsApp group with that man!' And I said to myself, right, that's going in to something. I don't know what, but it's just too good not to use. I've used that one a couple of times across different stories actually. Another time I heard a boy on a bus in Northumberland say to his friend with great wonder: 'I've been living here my whole life (probably ten years or something) and there's still roads here I've never even been down.'

There's another bit in *All Along the Echo* describing the wind that came from a conversation with a friend of mine on a ferry to Glasgow where I said something like 'Jaysus, that wind would shave you.' He came back with his own version and we were one-upping each other with 'that wind would rear your children for you', or whatever, all weekend. A version of that exchange went into the book and when I read it out at a launch in Dublin, I looked up and my friend was sitting there and he'd no memory of it and I'd never even realised that's where I'd taken it from.

SB: In both of your books, but particularly *The Earlie King...*, given its nature, you manage to create a strong sense of atmosphere. Was this something you were conscious of as you were writing, or did it develop organically?

DD: With *The Earlie King...* I had the world in my head before I had the story. For ages I wanted to write a book in an Ireland where it always rained and I would be constantly making notes. I had a little page in my notebook of pictures on repeat, things I didn't want the reader to see just once: neon; rusty cranes; train lines raised because of flooding. The plan was to build this world through repetition. You wouldn't see these things just once. You'd see a rusty crane every few pages, so when you were reading it, that was the geography of your mind when you thought about the book.

SB: The device of talk radio you employ in *All Along The Echo* is great way to explore any topic from every possible angle. Did you find this very freeing to write?

DD: Radio is proper democracy, it seems to me. It's allowing people of different belief systems, different opinions to share the same space. And that's getting pretty rare these days. It made for great fun with fiction because I don't have to feel bad about giving voice to anybody because it's accurate, no matter how dopey or politically deranged their opinions.

SB: And it gave you the opportunity to explore divided public opinion about the influx of people coming into a country with the returning Irish taking the place of an immigration argument.

DD: Yeah. I didn't set out to prove a point about casual racism or xenophobia, but each decision you make in a book has all these ricochets to it. I knew I wanted this idea of somewhere very close to Ireland being under severe threat, but I didn't think terrorism in Ireland was credible yet. I had lived in London, where it had happened, so I thought if that happened enough the Irish might start returning. And the ricochet of that is: what are people going to think about all these people coming home, and how are they going to integrate into a society where there's a homelessness crisis? What will people say about that? I saw a post on Reddit only yesterday asking for spare buggies or toys for Ukrainians. First comment under the post: what about people who want toys who are Irish?

SB: I know. It's so predictable.

DD: Yeah, it's devastatingly sad. But that's inevitable. And if that's inevitable, it's only accurate that it appears in the book.

SB: Was the idea of London being overwhelmed by terrorist attacks something that grew out of your own time there? Was it something you could feel in the collective consciousness of the city at the time?

DD: When the Paris attacks happened that straightened me in my seat. Like, you could die on your way to work. The scene in the theatre at the start was me having a shit attack about what it would have been like to be in the Bataclan that night. There's another scene where Tony interviews a guy who hid in a closet for hours. I worked in the building where that's based and nothing ever happened there, but I remember thinking what would I do? There was this closet where we took all the shelves out so we could hang our coats and I remember thinking, that's where I'm going. I'm not saying I was a nervous wreck walking around London but I was certainly wary about things happening and had contingency plans in my head.

SB: What are you working on now?

DD: A new novel. It's the story of a relationship, set partly in Cork, partly in Japan. And the same old thing with my books, it jumps around loads in form and time. So far anyway. There's also a natural disaster in it. For some reason the apocalypse is always at the edge of my work.

SB: And finally, could you give us a writing prompt for our readers?

DD:

1. Go outside. Feel the air on your face.
2. Listen to the sounds of the world.
3. Go back inside.
4. Admit something to yourself. Acknowledge something true about yourself that you've probably never been able to admit to yourself before. Be honest with yourself.
5. And accept it.
6. And sit with it for a few minutes.
7. Now give that realisation to a character in your fiction. They are at a swimming pool (don't know why or in what capacity). They are finally honest with themselves. Or maybe it comes out of the blue — the acknowledgment. They are at the swimming pool, facing themselves all of a sudden. What happens there in the swimming pool? Why are they at the pool? And where do they go next?
8. Write the scene.
9. Follow them.

Knocking on Wisdom's Door

by Zoey Sibanda

Bird

by Billy Fenton

Jock stood naked on the wall of the bridge, his clothes piled in a heap on the road beneath him. He faced the river, his arms spread out like an eagle, his bony legs bouncing up and down.

'Jump,' I yelled, 'jump.'

'Get off that wall and put your clothes on,' an old man who was passing shouted. The man's dog started to yap loudly. Two teenage girls stopped to watch, one holding the arm of the other as they giggled. Jock turned to face them.

'Fancy a bit of this?' he said.

'Jump,' I shouted, 'jump. Show 'em how it's done.'

I leaned over the wall, the river hurtling by. I looked up at Jock. He smiled, his hand moving over the stubble on his chin, a glint of evening sun on his gold earring. He turned back towards the river and raised his arms above his head.

'Get down,' the old man said. 'You'll kill yourself.'

'Time to fly,' Jock said.

He jumped, his body flying over the river, his arms spread out like a crucifix.

He had woken me that morning, a loud rap on my bedroom window. At first, I ignored it, but he persisted, adding my name to the rat-a-tat-tat. I fell out of bed and let him in.

'Time for a few bevvies, Seánín, up you get.'

He sat down on the couch, stretched out his legs, threw his packet of Old Holborn on to the coffee table.

'The head not too good?' he said laughing.

In the shower, the water cascaded over me. I turned the knob to blue.

'Looking spick and span, boy,' Jock said. 'There's a coffee for you.' He pointed to the worktop beside the cooker. 'And a wee rollie beside it.'

'What time is it?' I asked.

'Just after twelve.'

'What time did we leave the party last night?'

'I didn't, I slept on the floor behind the couch. When did you go?'

My mind struggled to find a memory but it couldn't, so I just shrugged.

'Must have been good then,' he laughed. 'Let's go.'

I slapped some marmalade on two slices of bread, grabbed a couple of bananas, the rollie Jock had made me, and followed him out the door.

The door of Clancy's on River Street was shut, a black piece of cloth with a death notice on it pinned to the door.

'I heard he wasn't well,' Jock said. 'He'll be missed.' He blessed himself as we continued up River Street.

'Let's try over there. Not a place I normally go into.' He pointed to the Bridge Bar across the road.

A one-room bar, grey counter with a red Formica top along one wall, an assortment of high stools, a scattering of tables and chairs, and walls devoid of any decoration. It reminded me of the pub in Kilclooney where my father used to drink. My mother used to send us there often, to get him to come home for his tea.

An elderly barman was fiddling with the remote control when we entered, two old men sat at the counter, a bag of messages sitting on the floor between them.

'Two pints of Guinness,' Jock said.

'Only bottles here, will that do?'

'If it gives the desired effect, anything will do.'

He placed two pint bottles and two glasses on the counter, turned back to the remote control. Restless images flickered overhead.

'There's never anything on,' said the barman.

'That's true,' said one of the old men.

Jock placed a ten pound note on to the counter.

I took a large gulp of Guinness, and my mind started to relax a little, like a weight of water pushing away a blockage on a river. I took another gulp.

'Doing the trick Seánín?' He slapped me on the back and turned to the two old men sitting at the bar.

'A wedding today?' The first old man was dressed in a suit, a carnation in his lapel, wisps of silver hair, a top hat beside him on the counter. He turned towards Jock.

'Who's getting married?' Jock said.

'I am,' the man said.

Jock looked at the barman for confirmation, but he was still engrossed in the remote control.

'Congratulations.' Jock shook the man's hand. 'And who's the lucky woman?'

'Nora Peg Gallagher. You might know her. She works in Brady's Drapers on High Street.'

Jock stroked his chin, looked at the other old man for help, but he was looking up at the TV.

'Where's Brady's?' he asked.

'Beside the Kildree Inn.'

Jock looked at me, shrugged his shoulders, smiled.

'She was twenty-two last week. I bought her a new dress for her birthday.'

Jock nodded, took another sip of his drink.

'She said she's going to wear it tonight. After the wedding.'

The man looked at his watch and said: 'I better be going, I'm due at the church in fifteen minutes.' He stood up, placed the top hat on his head and walked towards the door. 'I better not be late,' he said looking at his watch again.

The door shut behind him.

'He must be eighty?' Jock said.

'Eighty-five,' the other old man at the counter said.

'And he's getting married?'

'Fifty years ago he was. Nora never turned up. For the last few months he's started to turn up here every Saturday, as if he's living it all over again. Seems to make him happy, so what harm?'

'That's right,' the barman said. 'He's been lonely long enough, no harm in a bit of fantasy.'

'Yeah,' Jock said quietly, his face turning back towards the door.

We sat in silence for a few minutes, sipping our drinks, and I knew that he was thinking of his ex-fiancée, Sharon, and his heart was still hurting.

Jock spread the newspaper on the counter, opened the racing pages, reached for his drink and took a sip.

'Have you a pen and a piece of paper, Mick?' he said to the barman.

We were in the Morrissey's on Main Street, a new sort of place trying to look old, all wood and glass, covered in artefacts from a trip to a bar suppliers in Dublin. Five miles to Glockamara, thirty-five to Tír na nÓg, a couple in love sucking at woodbines like there was no tomorrow, a few musical instruments cluttering the upper shelves.

'Any tips doing the rounds, Mick?' Jock said.

'For the National?'

'Yeah, my one and only bet every year.'

'I'm sure.'

Jock placed the pen between his lips.

'There's a lot of talk about Sassy Lady and Man of Rockall, but I don't know, I'm not much of a betting man meself,' Mick said.

Jock pushed the paper in my direction and said: 'What's your bet, Seánie?'

'There all going for Dundee Lady, over in the bookie's,' a voice behind us said. 'And Whiskey Galore.'

'Ah, 'tis Puddy Ryan,' Jock said, 'sit down there and give us a bit of your craic. Mick, give Puddy whatever he's having.'

Puddy sat the other side of Jock. Short and overweight, a head of brown curls like a well-used floor mop. I turned my back on their chat and studied the paper.

'Well Seánie?' Jock finally said.

'I'll go with the Queen of Sheeba,' I said.

'No, no, no,' Puddy said, 'that's a hundred to one outsider. They never win.'

'They do,' I said, 'me father won in….'

'Never happens, don't be wasting your money.'

'Jock, which….?'

'Go for a horse like Dundee Lady, or better still King of Pluto. One of them is sure to win,' Puddy insisted.

'I'm heading across to the bookies. Jock, will I place a bet for you,' I said.

He scribbled on a piece of paper, handed me a twenty-pound note and said: 'Put a tenner on the Queen and a tenner on the Lady.' He winked at me and turned back towards Puddy.

'Don't be wasting…' Puddy's voice faded as the door swung shut behind me.

Puddy came back through the front door of Morrissey's like a clumsy Clint Eastwood, an unlit cigar protruding from the corner of his mouth.

'Ye should have listened to me lads.' He banged a wad of tens on to the counter. 'King of Pluto. Twenty to one. Two hundred smackeroonies.' He kissed the bundle of cash. 'Three Jamies, Mick.'

'Cheers boys,' he shouted, emptying the whiskey in a single swallow. Me and Jock did the same.

Jock called for three more.

Later that afternoon, after a few more pints, Jock and me left Morrissey's. We walked down Patrick's Lane towards the quay, stopped off in a deserted yard to roll a joint, then continued on to the riverbank. We sat down on a bench, stretched our legs across the footpath and I lit the joint. A man was kneeling in the cockpit of a river cruiser, the engine hatch open. He was cleaning an engine part with a piece of cloth. A lone heron waited for prey on the opposite bank. A ray of sun broke through the clouds, lighting up the old monastery on the hill. I waved to the man in the boat when he looked up.

'One day,' Jock said, 'I'm going to own a boat like that. And you and me, Seánie boy will sail down the river, out into the sea, and disappear - free as birds.'

We sat in silence for a few moments, passed the joint back and forth, watched the creases and swirls of the flow, the arches of the bridge, the heron making its way across the weir, cars passing on the South Quay, a group of teenagers looking for somewhere to go.

I took out a little plastic bag that I had stowed in my shirt pocket earlier that morning.

'What you got there, Seánie?'

I emptied two tabs of acid with the imprint of a dragon onto my palm.

'Where did you get those?' Jock smiled.

'A recent purchase. A Fog Hennessy special.'

I handed him one, swallowed the other.

He looked for a few moments at the tab, then raised his head and looked across the river. 'I called up to Sharon's place during the week,' he said, 'thinking enough time had passed since she broke it off. I promised to turn over a new leaf if she came back to me - take it easier on the drink.' He inhaled the last of the joint, blew the smoke back out through his nose, threw what remained into the river. 'She said she'd heard it all before. Too many times. Said I had a problem. Now, I do like a good drink, a good party, I'll admit that, but a problem?'

The heron on the weir took to air. We watched it fly over the surface of the river, over the bridge, until it dipped back down and disappeared.

Jock shook his head, looked down at the tab, hesitated, then popped it into his mouth, and swallowed. 'Next stop Zanzibar,' he said.

Zanzibar was part of the Central Hotel, and it never opened until six, so when we got there it was still closed.

'Another half an hour,' I said.

'Kiely's for a quick one,' Jock suggested.

Two women sat at the bar; three large shopping bags parked at their feet. A man was snoring at the end of the counter, his head buried in his arms.

'Well girls,' Jock said.

'Hello Jock,' the blonde woman said.

Jock leaned on the bar beside her and ordered two pints. 'And give the girls whatever they're having.'

'No thanks, we're just about to go.'

'Sure we'll have one more,' the black-haired woman said looking in my direction. 'Aren't you always waiting for him to come home, Rose? Can't he wait for you for a change?'

They both laughed.

The women were familiar to me, but I didn't know them well. Both worked as cashiers in Costigan's Supermarket. In their forties, fashionably dressed, thick coat of make-up, red lips, the tired faces of a hard life.

'Who's your friend?' the black-haired woman asked.

'Seán Boyle,' Jock said.

She took my hand in both of hers, looked directly at me: 'Hazel's my name. So, pleased to meet you, Seán.' I could smell her perfume, the scent of her body, and felt myself blush as she slowly released my hand.

Behind us there was a loud bang, then another. The sleeping man had woken and was beating his glass on the counter, looking for a drink. He had a face like a bruised beetroot, his clothes well worn, his words barely decipherable.

'You've had enough, Tadhg,' the barman said. 'I'll call you a taxi.' He reached for the phone. The man banged the glass twice more, wheezed like a deflating balloon, then slumped back onto the counter.

'You heard Sharon and me split up?' Jock said.

Both women nodded. Rose put her hand on his arm and said: 'What happened Jock?'

'This,' he said, and he held up his drink.

'Oh, sure you don't drink any more than the rest of us?' Hazel said.

There was a groan from the corner, and Tadhg banged his glass again.

'Now, that's real drinking,' Hazel laughed as we all looked in Tadhg's direction.

'She got it in her head that we should buy a house,' Jock continued, 'Wanted us to start saving. Save what? I said.'

'Don't you have your name down with the council? You'd have a good chance of getting one of their new houses in Friary Grove once they're finished,' Hazel said.

'That's what I told her, but she wants us to buy. Said it'd be great to own our own place.'

'Ah, she's losing the run of herself. Isn't she, Rose?'

'Mmm,' Rose said.

Jock raised his glass to his mouth and emptied it slowly, and then turned and walked towards the door.

'I'm off to Zanzibar,' he said. 'Are ye coming?'

'Why not?' Hazel said. 'You coming, Rose?'

'You're trying to get me divorced, Hazel Dalton.'

As we crossed the Square, a light canvas of rain pulsed like a million diamonds across the square, buildings hung like shadows behind the veil, cars whispered by. In the little grassy space in the centre of the square, I stopped for a moment to enjoy the coolness of the fine rain, the colours of the flowers, the flutter of leaves, a spring blue through a break in the clouds. The drugs were doing their work, and I suddenly knew I was out of it.

The noise of a revving engine, a cloud of black smoke, disturbed me, and I continued towards Zanzibar. A modern mess of mirrors and red, and loud music. Jock and the two women were sitting at a table tucked in at one of the front windows.

'Where were you?' Jock said.

'What do you mean?'

'We left Kiely's a good while ago. We thought you were lost.'

I shrugged and reached for my drink.

'He needs looking after,' Hazel said. Her hand slipped briefly around my waist. I let myself lean into her. Jock looked at me and smiled. Rose looked away.

'Let's go and put something better on the juke box,' Rose said to Hazel.

'Good gear that,' I said to Jock.

'Yeah, happy days, made to order.'

'Be careful with Hazel,' Jock said.

I turned back towards the bar.

'She's married.'

'I'll take my chances.'

I pushed out my half-finished cigarette, headed towards the gents.

Johnny Cash was singing about hating every inch of San Quentin when I got back, and the two women were singing along. I called for another round.

'Not for me,' Rose said.

'Ah go on, Rose, one for the road,' Hazel said.

'No, I'm for home, it's been a long day.'

'Ah, one more. Get her one, Seán.'

Rose stood to leave.

'Where's our bags?' Rose said.

They both looked around.

'Ah shit, we must have left them in Kiely's,' Hazel said.

'Don't worry, I'll go and get them,' I offered.

'He's such a honey,' Hazel said, and she reached over and kissed me on the cheek. As I headed out I heard her say: 'we'll have that drink while we're waiting.'

When I got back with their bags, Jock was missing. At first, I thought he'd gone to the toilet, but after a few minutes I asked Rose.

'Sharon came in, and he followed her down the back.'

We sang along to what the jukebox gave, clinking our glasses, talking about things I can't remember.

'Seán,' Jock's voice called.

He was standing by the door of the pub. I walked over to him.

'I'm heading over the bridge to Kavanagh's,' he said. He was agitated. I looked towards the back of the bar. Sharon was sitting at a table, talking animatedly to a friend. They looked once in our direction.

'You coming?' he said, and he left. I walked back towards our table, reached for my drink and drank steadily until it was empty. I looked at the bar. At Hazel. At the door. Then back at the bar.

I followed Jock.

Jock fell with a huge splash on to the river. I hung over the wall, waited for his body to rise from the muddy flow. His bare back, the stream of his long hair, his face submerged, his arms out to the side. Not a trace of movement.

'Jock,' I shouted. 'Jock.'

I clambered on to the wall to go after him, but a couple of men who had jumped from a passing car stopped me. I punched wildly to get away, but they pinned me to the wall.

Another man jumped over the wall and into the river. I watched as I squirmed against their bodies.

'Jock, Jock…let me fucking go.'

The current was taking Jock rapidly downstream.

'Jock…'

Then he sank.

The man swam to where Jock disappeared, dived a few times. His head growing smaller in the water as the current took him downstream.

It's almost two weeks since Jock drowned. Almost every night I wake, the image of his naked body flying through the air, expanding and shrinking, like a camera zooming in and out. The sound of thunder as he hits the water. There's an ache in my belly when I wake. Most times I can't get back to sleep. I sit at my bedroom window and watch the shimmer of streetlights, the shadows of this sleeping town, listen to the tap-tap of rain against my window, my last words to Jock echoing through my brain.

After leaving Zanzibar that night, I caught up with him on the bridge. He had stopped in the centre and was leaning over the stone wall. The sun had broken through the clouds, and I could feel the heat of it against my face, every detail of the world around me leaping into focus as the acid continued to unfold its story.

'Remember when we were boys, we used to jump off the bridge?' Jock had said as he looked down into the river. 'Like we were birds. And we'd climb out on those steps, and run back here and fly again, over and over. Like the whole summer would never end.'

'Go on. Do it,' I said.

'Jump?' Jock said with a grin.

'Yeah, jump,' I laughed, 'jump.'

object permanence

by Ewan Monaghan

you brushed against my life,
left a vivid lily-pollen stain

& I did not know how to sweep
this powdered ochre from my sleeve,

a coral stripe at the wrist
like a mouth open & still calling out.

I remember your damp hair
left a helix, tumbling DNA,

a spectre, a condensed curl
on the passenger side glass:

my glamorous wraith, my familiar.
I drove that print around for months

delicately, as if delivering a Gentileschi.
Me, the restorer who'd seen the x-ray

below the oils, the pencil sketch
where the lover's fingers still touch.

La Chapelle Secrète

by Tony Evans

A good death

by Katie Oliver

The appointment comes through quickly: urgent
referral, two weeks' time. I am too young to die

like those tragic queens before me.
I conjure thick needles, scalpels slicing

through my flesh. I am Anne Boleyn
I have only a little neck.

My grip on life is fragile
as a crown: it cannot rest

on severed heads. I'll hang on
until my nails are bloody, staving off

the sword's silent rush; the dull thunk
of an axe. *The work of a moment.*

I am fabulous in my peril:
coordinate my mask with my outfit

and pencil on a fierce brow.
I am Katherine Howard

clinging to my jewels, requesting a block
to rehearse my execution, chest heaving

beneath a bodice of red velvet.
When I consider the lump in my breast

(protruding, as yet undefined)
I just want to say

that if it comes to it
I would like to make

a good death.

Filament

by Joshua Jones Lofflin

It's a single strand of copper, stripped from one of the telephones in Mouse's collection. He and his brother have scavenged over a dozen from the office his brother cleans; gears and springs and earpieces cover the only table in his flat. The wire stretches from a watch Mouse bought himself with money that was supposed to go toward textbooks — a quartz action Casio with a liquid crystal display. The wire's other end connects to a lumpy package wrapped twice in duct tape, then taped again to the underside of the café table. The watch's display counts down, one second at a time. When it gets to 0:00, a signal will travel along the copper filament, pushing electrons down its length at almost half the speed of light. There won't be enough time to breathe, to blink, to form a thought.

It will be big, Mouse tells Sadya and takes her hand. He wanted to tell his brother about her; after last night, he thinks he still might, but she made him promise he wouldn't.

How big? Sadya asks, but Mouse only shrugs. She pulls her hand away, says, What do you mean you don't know. Are we too close?

They're in her beige Opel across the street and two storefronts down from the café. Close enough they can watch the comings and goings but not so near they'll arouse the suspicions of the bodyguards standing at its door. The two men smoke Turkish cigarettes. Their eyes drift across the hatchback but don't linger — this is a safe street in a safe neighborhood. The café owner, a large chested widow from Armenia, can be trusted. She brings the men pastries and pats their bellies saying they need a woman to fatten them up. She inhales the scent of their tobacco and scans the street with them and frowns when she sees Sadya behind the wheel waiting. She never learned to drive and doesn't trust girls who do.

She'd been in the kitchen when Sadya sat at the table unspooling the duct tape beneath the checkered table cloth. When she emerged with Sadya's tea, she scowled at the girl's eye shadow, the short hair, the dress that rose easily above the knee. No, she didn't like the look of the girl, the way her hand trembled as she drank her tea. She was glad to see the girl leave. She didn't notice her throwing up beside the car.

That was just before the Baker arrived. He's older and frailer looking than Mouse expected. He leans on a silver-tipped cane, his right knee stiff. It's not a war injury, he tells people who assume it's from shrapnel. Just age. Arthritis. But I do my part, in my own way.

Five minutes later, the Butcher arrives, not in a glossy black Mercedes like the Baker, but in a dusty Renault, almost identical to the taxi Mouse's uncle drove for fifteen years until a mortar pierced his bedroom window, as if aimed by God. The Butcher lumbers out of the back of the sedan and enters the café where he embraces the Baker and kisses him on each cheek. Then they both sit, their knees framing the small package taped beneath the table.

The Butcher has been shot three times over the course of his sixty-eight years — four if you count the bullet that removed the tip of his left ear, not that he ever does. He's no longer the barrel-chested soldier of those days and has grown fat and jowly; his wife's convinced that it will be diabetes that kills him. He sometimes loses feeling in his toes, and he doesn't notice when his knee brushes the edge of the package and jostles the watch — its display ticking below ten minutes.

Mouse's leg won't stop shaking. Sadya clamps a hand on it and tells him everything will be fine. It's a skinny leg, a boy's leg. The night before she'd marveled at his fragile, birdlike bones, the way he trembled as she touched him, the way his own fingers traced around the scars on her back, never quite touching them. He'd told her he was falling for her, and she laughed and kissed his ear and said happy birthday after he came, even though it's not till June, even though he'll never reach it. It will take authorities two weeks to identify his remains from the gold tooth in the smoldering ruins of his flat. They will publicly declare it a gas explosion. They will arrest his brother and break his fingers and sodomize him until he tells them everything he thinks they want to hear.

How's your health? Is your family well? the Butcher asks, and the Baker tells him about his newest granddaughter — his fifth — and brags about how fat her cheeks are. He hopes to be a great-grandfather soon, if only his eldest will come back from England and settle down. The Butcher nods knowingly. His family isn't as large, smaller now since the death of his son. He takes a Polaroid of his two grandchildren from his breast pocket and shows it to the Baker.

Beautiful. Both boys, the Baker says approvingly and sets the photo between them. Less than an inch of wood separates it from the package taped beneath. You must spoil them, the Baker says, and the Butcher shrugs and sips his coffee. He drinks it with sugar since his wife isn't here to chide him. He slathers butter on a sweetened bun.

Flies buzz lazily over the table, but nobody complains; they're everywhere this time of year, in this part of the city. Other than the two men, the owner, and the flies, the café is empty, and for that Sadya is grateful. Outside, a woman in a headscarf walks down the street, approaching the smoking bodyguards. Sadya checks her watch. Walk faster, she whispers. Don't slow down.

The Butcher gets down to business, tells the Baker what he needs, how much, where to route the funds. I know it's a lot, he says, but this operation, it's important. No, it's essential.

The Baker nods and stirs his coffee with a miniature spoon even though the sugar has dissolved. A fly lands on the back of his hand. He brushes it off.

Can you do it? the Butcher asks.

It will be difficult. The embargoes, they slow everything down. But yes, I can do it. I only need time, the Baker replies. By his knees, the Casio's display flashes 0:55, 0:54, 0:53.

The fly settles beside the Polaroid between them and begins to probe the table for crumbs. After this, we will crush the embargoes, the Butcher says, and he slams his hand down on the fly with such force that the table rattles. The café owner jumps as if a gunshot went off, almost spilling her carafe of coffee. The bodyguards glance inside to see that everything is fine, then resume their smoking. Beneath the table, the copper filament dangles lifelessly, no longer attached to the blinking watch.

Sadya checks the time again and again. She yells at Mouse, hits him, shouts at him to get out of the car, to do something, anything, that they'll never get this chance again. Mouse pleads with her to stop, says she's making a scene, that the bodyguards are watching, and it's true, they are. The Butcher's bodyguard stubs out his cigarette and takes a step forward, his hand already reaching for the pistol beneath his jacket. But then the Opel pulls away, and the Baker's bodyguard says, Relax, it's nothing. He will remain employed by the Baker for three more years and then, after the Baker dies in Bern from heart failure, will work for the Baker's son, but it won't be the same. The son is arrogant and cold and barely remembers the bodyguard's name.

The Butcher will outlive his friend by another twelve years, despite his diabetes, despite a cancer diagnosis, despite two more attempts on his life — the last one an IED that takes his bodyguard's leg. Instead, he will die in his seaside villa, in his sleep, from an aneurism, and his photograph will be paraded around the city by thousands of white-robed sympathizers.

Sadya will be in America by then with a different name and longer hair. She'll see the news next to her American husband as they flip through the cable channels. Go back, she'll tell him, and he'll flick back to CNN where they'll see photos of the Butcher in fatigues, from when he was younger, from before his ear was shot.

Did you know him? her husband will ask, in that stupid way he does even though he knows she never talks about the past or how she lost her three fingers or the boy she once knew who she couldn't remember if she loved or not.

No, she'll say. Then the screen will cut to Anderson Cooper, to some celebrity scandal, to a promo for next season of *Dancing with the Stars*, to a commercial for erectile dysfunction.

journal / measuring grief
by Sodiq Oyèkàmí

iii.

today, i quit my job at the national theatre.

x.

even with this pen in my hand, i still weigh 61kg.
even after the therapy, a bullet still trails me in my dreams.
even in my dreams /   in this silence / this silence / silence…

even in this spill of light, my body is still halved by / with darkness.

v.

look how i'm failing ~~beautifully~~ again at holding myself from shattering
like the mirror taped to the greenroom wall.

i look inwardly

        & see nothing but a wounded boy.

even with my eyes closed, i know the etymology of my grief.
ask me, & i'll raise my middle finger towards a country / a bullet.

i.

today, i'm 23.
    & i mostly dream in black & white.

vi.

it is autumn in my body again. my joy is skinning away.

iv.

slowly, all my flowers wither. except for the cactuses.

& as if a dress rehearsal for a forthcoming tragedy,

a thorn pricks my thumb.

ix.

at the therapist: a dialogue.

- how are you?
- <an automatic reply> i'm fine.
- it's okay if your heart needs more time
  to accept what your mind already knows.
  some lesions? need time to heal…
  <a brief pause> how are you S?
- i'm —   /

see how grief trans –

mutes me into silence.

vii.

~~<a silence the size of a bullet>~~

xi.

look —

past the margins of this page;
past the cyclorama of this stage;

past the sightlines.
& if you look right through enough, there is a boy —
living monastically — making tea from dandelion roots.

ii.

somedays, i break the fourth wall /   & ask my audience for help.
believe me, some worriment does not need a deus ex machina.
you just need to step right out of it.   like this.

xii.

& this is my mouth's font of saying:

see, i used to have a sweet smile & a contagious laugh too;
stood on a rostrum of happiness without tripping.
i used to be a part of this grand bliss
& never missed my cue…

but now, i stand close to the apron, empty,

                  empty,

                      empty & waiting for the finale.

     viii.

it is always autumn in my body / ever since i lost my brother.

Hush

by Martins Deep

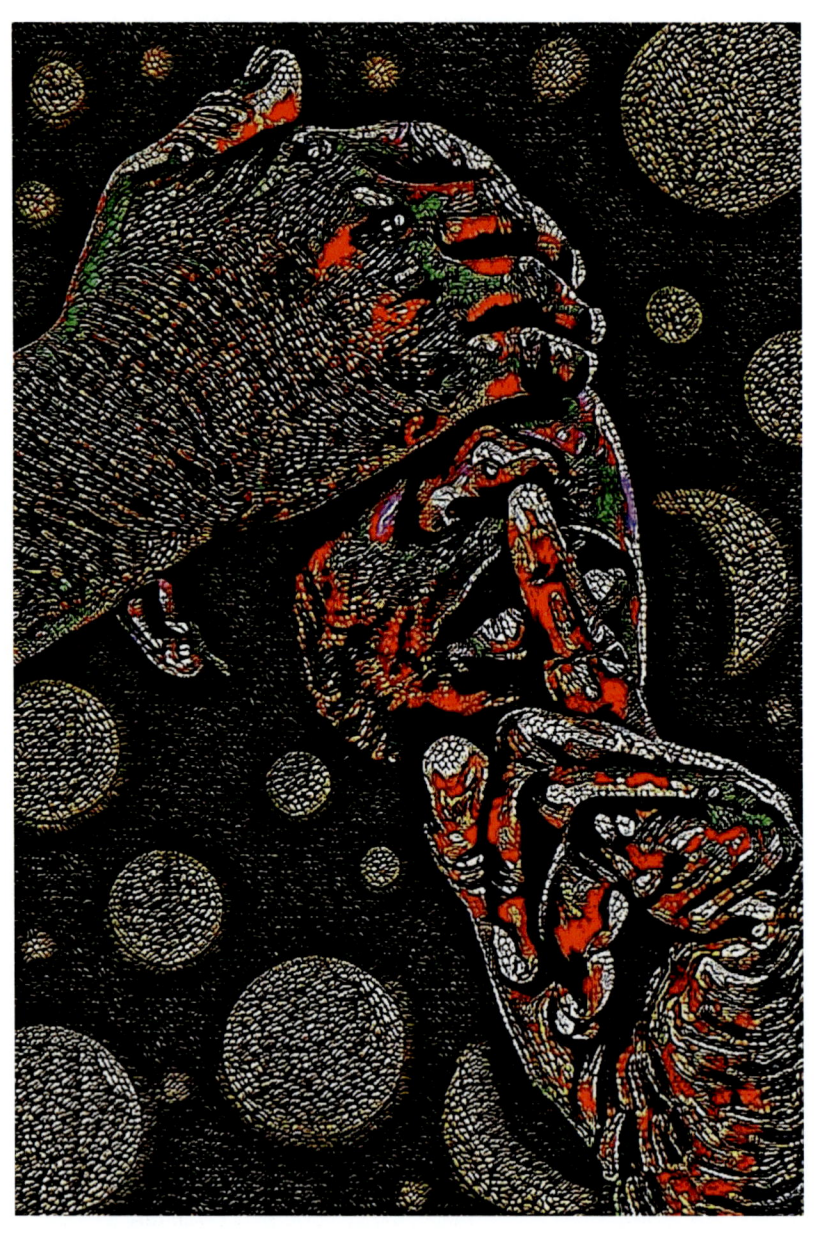

My First Garden

by Thea Petrou

I have been taking a writing class. The instructor has asked us each to hand in roughly two pages of our own writing so that it can be workshopped by the group. That is the problem with these writing classes. At least I have a couple of weeks to think about it. It is much worse when we are invited to conjure something up in under ten minutes for one of those on-the-spot imaginative exercises. The panic. All the more intense for being short-lived. The rush to think of a not-too-silly idea. Then the relief when I think enough of the other attendees might volunteer before me, enough for me not to have to raise my own hand.

I am more of a translator than a writer. The book I am working on now is about two women: a photographer, who died young after leading a troubled life, and her archivist, who collates her vast collection of photographs and curates the artist's only major exhibition, posthumously. Their voices are different. The archivist-curator writes the book in pared down language that I find easy to slip into — simple sentences that seem sometimes to stop short, leaving her reader to suppose what comes next. And there are lots of clauses separated by commas instead of conjunctions, inviting me to infer the relationship between the events they recount. Her subject is the work of the artist, some of the life around that work, and glimpses into her own experience piecing it all together in the archive. But she writes with uncertainty, keeping biographical accounts and the varying anecdotes they produced at a distance, preferring her own unreliability as narrator and building her book on the speculation that thrives in the interstices. Perhaps this is because she does not want to speak for the woman who is gone. And as her translator, I feel this fear of misrepresenting her in turn, of faltering in her voice.

The artist speaks in the book through extracts of the letters she had written to friends. I struggle technically with these sections. Her language is eccentric, dramatic, exhibiting a flair and a brilliance that take me hours longer to create than the rest of the book, even though her passages constitute only a fraction of the text. I am always glad to be the archivist again, sorting through the material of someone else's life.

This is not so bad, see. I have managed a couple of paragraphs. But it is easy to write about books – that has been another of my other jobs. I can begin where the book begins, pad out an introduction with the anecdotes about the writer we have all already heard, then show off with some of the lesser-known facts. I am not left contemplating the vast dimensions of the blank white page until two days before the deadline.

The artist was bilingual. She describes living between French and English, and in the diary she wrote, published after her death, she sometimes translates her experiences between the two languages: love, photography, pain. In the translations from one language to the other, something always shifts, and I sense that she never felt settled, whether in her country of birth or the place she moved to for a new life with her husband.

I have always said I was bilingual. Growing up, a few members of my family spoke in Greek, but at home we spoke mostly in English. The result is a mix of rudimentary phrases, colloquial Cypriot expressions, and a repertoire of terms used in moments of rage. I have ended up with a Greek that is *broken*. Isn't it funny that we think of language as a faulty object in this way when it is we that do not fit comfortably within its contours? Now I work with French literature and poetry, and I translate from French and Italian into English. When someone asks me a question in Greek, I have a strange impulse to answer in Italian. Italian is the language I have spent the least years with, my most recent acquisition, and yet I have a firmer grasp of its grammatical architecture than I do of Greek, and it slips more effortlessly off my tongue. In Greek grammar I stumble over articles and word endings. I search for words that never materialise, leaving me floundering.

We had always assumed my grandmother could not speak any English. Or not much. She had worked in factories making pencils, occasionally gifting us cherished wooden boxes whose lids slid open to reveal rainbows of colour. She loved gardening and flowers. At family gatherings, we joked that she might be eavesdropping on our gossiping, coded in a language foreign to her, but we were all surprised when she responded confidently in English to nurses during her last stay in hospital. Since her death, I have regretted the shallowness of our conversations and the questions I never formulated in spoken words. What was it like to travel all those miles by ship, and to arrive to no welcome? Who did you meet and talk to in the days that journey took? As I look around, I wonder what essentials I would pack from my home full of books, shoes and comfortable furniture. And I feel breathless at the enormity of the decision she took.

In last week's class we learnt about the role of dialogue and direct speech in nonfictional narrative, the ways it can tell a story without you telling the story. And I search around for some clever snippet of conversation that I might add to my writing, like a tiny, brilliant jewel – illuminating, reflective, enjoyed, even, for its own presence. But I cannot think of anything that would serve these functions.

Though they came to London separately, she later had my grandfather as a companion. I balk at how young she was when they were married, just a child. I remember him as a kind and smiling old man, pressing a pound coin into the palm of my hand. In his children's memories, he was not always so pleasant. On our first visit to the house after he died and was buried, my grandmother cried: the sudden realisation that he was not there as we carried on with our routine, with life.

At my grandmother's funeral, my cousin's speech elicited a giggle when she recalled my grandmother's *new lease of life* on being widowed. In those last few years, she had made friends and gone on trips — independent for the first time.

While today some readers are turned off by the *second-hand feel* of a translated story, in the past the translated quality of a text was a sought-after trait. Something to do with the higher value of languages *other* than your own, the fashionable cultures that readers wanted to emulate.

I recently read an article about pseudo-translation. While a translation implies the existence of a source text (written in another language, another culture), a relationship tying the source text to the target text, and the transfer of features that both texts will share following translation, the pseudo-translation has none of these. It is always already written in the target language, created in that language as an original work, but made to look like a translation, maybe through ostentatious (bogus) translator's notes, references to the made-up original, or obvious caricatured stereotypes. Ironically, these are traits we would never really see in translation, which usually aspires to produce a text that does not directly refer to its other, earlier existence, and which often transposes events more subtly from one culture into the another. Until quite recently a translated book would not even show the translator's name on its cover.

I cannot stop thinking about these strange texts — pseudo-translations — that reach beyond their own boundaries and pretend to be tied to other languages and cultures. Imagine taking away every part of the translation process: the lists of synonyms that I come back to again and again, narrowing them down further on each re-reading; the immersion in someone else's experience or way of thinking, and the words they use to tell this, sometimes so draining that after a day of translating I feel disorientated when I finally speak to another person or encounter the flickering noise of the TV; and, the close reading that is the first step in every translation. All you have left, then, is that blank page.

I do not have to scroll down far to see the bottom of my own second page now. It will soon be time to tie everything together, to explain the connection between the characters in my short story. I will probably have to account for bringing the small piece of my family history into my reflection on translation, for the unlikely parallel between my grandmother and the artist-archivist duo that are taking up my days. Perhaps it will be disappointing to admit that I simply thought of my grandmother in the early hours of a sleepless night this week, when translation, language and belonging were themes that were already on my mind.

Early on in the book I am translating, the writer explains how the hours spent sorting through the archive had given her a false sense of proximity to her subject, leaving her feeling more keenly the danger of losing her focus on the artist's work and slipping into the realms of biography. She writes that she prefers the first-person narrative pronoun 'I' to all other voices, its 'modesty', its honesty, the promise of ignorance that comes with its subjectivity forming a level of protection against an insistence that her subject 'was this, or that'. I have felt myself at ease in her first-person account — her dilemma familiar to me — though always at a remove.

On reading my translation so far, a friend described it as 'one of those quiet books'. I wondered if a translation (or a translator) was always quiet. When translators win prizes and awards, is it because their work speaks more or less loudly than the source text? Is it something to do with the styling of the ties to the 'original' and the transferred features? Does it stand out, or stand apart?

I think I am probably done. I feel compelled to write something about my grandmother having led a quiet life. Quiet but brave. And maybe a little sad. Or maybe I feel sad that I will never share with her the love I have found in growing my first garden.

The Dogs in the Streets of Mariupol

by Mary O' Donnell

They missed the last train out of town
when their owners fled
with children, a favourite toy,
a backpack. Empty-bellied now,
a scrawn of rib and hip
as their skin loosens, they wander
bewildered through the city.

Even the ground is angry,
their paws slit by broken streets,
where they smell necrotic flesh.
No-one will call out, kindly
urge them to lie at evening
by the flickering hearth
as their owners sip coffee.
Nobody tells them what to do.

At night, they curl in a chill
of blown brickwork.
Their nostrils and ears quiver
in the silence
from the bombed hospital.

In sleep, they tremble,
the dogs
        who have missed
          the train.

Smoke

by Mary O' Donnell

though his family beg him
the old man refuses to leave.
his grand-daughter weeps
from within a zipped red puffa
sees how *Dido* will not budge
the walls on his house are cracked
at night frost
a white snake in his room
his morning coffee grows weaker,
more transparent, his belly
bubbling with slow hunger
the need for air drives him out
but his local shop
is a gap in a grinning street,
the old water boiler crushed
and smashed vegetables warn him away
like jeering alphabets

on the horizon   smoke
on nearby streets   smoke
behind those he meets —
the ones who stayed —
a darkness in human form
slowly   looms
over their heads,
as if hatred had legs and arms
an expressionless face —

Dunnock

by Aileen Hunt

Peadar Maloney heads off to the bog wearing his father's overcoat — an old shapeless thing of uncertain colour. Under his arm, he's carrying a brown paper parcel tied with string.

The September air is crisp, but Peadar is already starting to sweat. He slows his step for a minute, then changes his mind and speeds up again. Over the hill he goes, through the gap in the gorse and past Murphy's rusted gate. Not far now.

At the bend, he meets Mick Reilly's father, Joe. His heart sinks.

'Brisk day,' he says, and Reilly's rheumy eyes take in the parcel. Peadar brazens it out. 'Any luck at the mart this year?' he asks. Reilly thrusts his hands in his pockets.

'Sure you know yourself,' he answers. 'Good and bad.'

'That's the way of it,' Peadar agrees, and steps around his neighbour. 'I'm off for a walk before tea,' he says, leaving Reilly two additional mysteries to ponder in his nightly rosary — the absence of Peadar's dog and the contents of Peadar's parcel.

As soon as he's out of sight, Peadar takes a big lugful of air. What now? Reilly will tell everyone he meets about their encounter. Peadar should probably get home, save himself the trouble of having to answer awkward questions the next time he's at the pub. But he can't stop now. All week, he's been thinking about the bog — the great empty stretch of it, the sudden pools that appear and disappear beneath his feet. The perfect place.

The sun emerges from behind a cloud and Peadar takes its watery warmth as encouragement. He hasn't slept since he found the suitcase in the attic, hasn't been able to concentrate on anything but the trip to the bog.

He thought he'd go early in the week, steal out when his father was down the village or round at Sullivan's. But it's Friday now. The days slipped by in their usual monotony. Milking in the morning, the plink of milk against metal a type of conversation. Painting the byre with slick, dripping whitewash. Sloshing water over the muck and cow pats in the yard. Always another job to do. Another reason to wait.

At night, Peadar sat in the chair that used to be his mother's, pretending to read in the yellow light of the kerosene. But his eyes refused to focus, skipping instead to the shadows flickering on the flags beside his father's feet.

'Will you have a drop?' his father asked, but Peadar shook his head. His dreams were strange enough.

A gust of wind in the hedgerow, and the startled squeak of a dunnock. Peadar lifts his head. Almost there! He quickens his pace, feels the familiar squelch under his boots. In front of him, the bog widens into its drab, brown nature. He pushes in, past a handful of ricks waiting to be brought home; a silver flask forgotten on top of the peat. On into the centre, as far from the road as he can get.

Yesterday, one of the sheep got stuck on a neighbour's fence.

'Hold him still,' his father had barked, tearing the wool from the barbed wire with his bare hands. 'Bloody sheep. They've no sense.'

Peadar held the sheep by the shoulder, tried to reassure it through the firmness of his hands. He wanted to touch the pink oval of its ear, to see how the velvet felt on his calloused hands, but his father slapped the animal on the rump, roared at it to get lost for God's sake. Together, they watched it take off across the field.

'It's a wonder some animals survive at all,' his father said. 'Always trying to escape.' He coughed a brittle cough and turned towards the house.

Peadar sets his parcel down beside a small pool, stretches tall and spins in a slow circle. The empty bog sweeps away from him.

He listens for low voices or the tell-tale suck of a boot in the mud, hears only the click, click, of a grouse hiding in heather. He pats his trouser pocket, checks to see if the box of Maguires' he took from the kitchen table is still there.

And now Peadar kneels on the wet ground and tugs at the string around the parcel, but his hands are shaking, and it takes three attempts to pull the string free of its knot. He folds back the brown paper, his heart hammering through his father's coat, and he can hardly look now, he remembers it so well. The surprise when he stumbled across the suitcase in the attic, the quick peak inside, the slowing of his breath when he realised what he was seeing.

He's going to be disappointed, he's sure of it, his memory bound to have tricked him. But his eyes widen when he sees the clothes again. The colours! Pink and lilac. Silvery blue. Raspberry.

He reaches down and takes the rainbow in his hand, flicks it into the air. So light! He holds the silk against his chest, feels it flutter in his hands. He waits for just a second before looking down at his reflection in the pool, and his smile is wide and sudden as the Shannon.

And now a groan rises from Peadar, an anguished cry like the bellow of a cow calling for her calf. He bunches the clothes into a ball, piles them onto a rock. What was he thinking coming here? He should never have opened that suitcase.

He fumbles in his pocket for the matches, strikes the head against the rough edge of the box. The clothes burn slowly, their colors darkening until they match the black-brown murk of the bog. Peadar stands over the shrivelling ashes and his father's coat hangs like a shadow from his shoulders.

Ciao Bella

by Serena Piccoli

Notes on Art & Photography

Zoey Sibanda – *Knocking on Wisdom's Door*

Oil painting, photography, digital collaging.

Martins Deep – *Hush*

Photography, digital collaging.

'Hush represents a digital continuation of an art piece begun with local rice and grits of other local grains to illustrate how we are comprised of fragments, from organelles that make up cells, to molecules, to individual experiences. The covered face with a hand is anthropomorphic and represents all the forces that make creation possible, with the index finger on the lips as a sign of the power of silence over our opinions and philosophical and religious beliefs.'

Tony Evans – *La Chapelle Secrète*

Photography, montage.

'On holiday in the Herault region of France, we discovered La Chapelle Secrète (The Secret Chapel) while walking a gorge. Derelict but in good condition, the stone altar remained in the nave covered in handwritten letters, floral offerings and fruit, some decaying and some fresh, as though the place was still visited by the relatives of lost loved-ones, or ghosts, perhaps. The overlay images were made in the hope it would retain the feel of a whispered past.'

James Harris – *Fiery Dawn*

Photography.

'I took this photo just after 6.00 am on 15th August 2021. I take a walk through my local park every weekend, with my camera ready for anything remarkable or beautiful that catches my eye. That morning the "golden hour' lived up to its name; part of the heathland looked alight between the trees. The sunrise and summer morning mist combined perfectly for a scene that I knew was going to make an amazing image as soon as the shutter clicked.'

E.E. King – *The Discus Player*

Acrylic on canvas (three panels) photographed by Eric Wallengren.

'I originally photographed an art class at Berkeley University. They were painting a nude but I changed it to The Discus Player. It is a triptych of panels and the artists are painting the discus player but they are making it into self-portraits. Art is a reflection of the artists. Painters see themselves in their subject. On both side panels the art is taking over the artists, reaching through the canvas and possessing the artists as all good art does.'

Serena Piccoli – *The Waiting Chair*

Photography.

'I took the photo with my Canon EOS M5 in Chester, England, a city that I love. When I saw the chair I imagined it was waiting for a person to sit there; a person finally coming back from a far away place, or returning after a long absence (stuck somewhere remote due to the pandemic, or being kept in hospital, or someone trapped in a prison cell). It's a joyful piece. The person is about to return and will bring joy with them again.'

Special thanks to Tadhg Crowley, Senior Curator at The Glucksman, UCC, who acted as visual-art consultant.

Contributors

Eniola Abdulroqeeb Arówólò is a Nigerian writer and a member of the Frontiers Collective His works have appeared in Fourth River Review, Rulerless, Perhappened, Kissing Dynamite, Lumiere Review, Temz Review, Afritondo, Better than Starbucks, Rough Cut Press, Brittle Paper, and elsewhere. Currently, James Baldwin is his most-cherished writer.

Jan Carson is the Belfast based author of two short story collections, three novels and two micro-fiction collections. Her novel, The Fire Starters won the EU Prize for Literature for Ireland in 2019 and the Kitschies Prize for Speculative Fiction 2020 and was shortlisted for the Dalkey Book Prize 2020. Her third and most recent novel, The Raptures was published in January 2022.

Martins Deep (he/him) is an Urhobo poet based in Zaria. He is a photographer, digital artist, & currently an undergraduate student of Ahmadu Bello University, Zaria.

Danny Denton is a writer of fiction, including the novels The Earlie King & The Kid In Yellow and All Along The Echo. He lectures on writing at University College Cork and is a contributing editor to The Stinging Fly.

Leah Duarte is a Portuguese-Canadian poet. A graduate of the University of Toronto's MA in English program, her thematic interests are shaped by her experiences grappling with diasporic distance. Her recent work has appeared or is forthcoming in The /tɛmz/ Review, untethered magazine, and elsewhere. Find her on Twitter @llduart_.

Nidhi Zak/Aria Eipe is a poet, pacifist and fabulist. Founder of the Play It Forward Fellowships, she serves as poetry editor at Skein Press and Fallow Media, and contributing editor with The Stinging Fly. Auguries of a Minor God, her debut poetry collection, was published by Faber in 2021.

Tony Evans is a Welsh illustrator and animator. In 2019 he won a London Seasonal Short Film Festival award for his animation and was also nominated for best indie film score at the London International Film Festival. His work has featured in various places, including the cover of British Horizons Magazine.

Dean Fee is a writer and editor based in Donegal. His work has appeared in The Stinging Fly, The Dublin Review, The Tangerine, and more. He is currently working on a novel.

Billy Fenton lives in Tramore, Co Waterford. His work has been published in the Irish Times, Poetry Ireland Review, Irish Independent, The North, Orbis, Crannóg, Honest Ulsterman, Abridged, Acumen, and many others. He was shortlisted for a Hennessy Award in 2018, and was appointed poet laureate for Carrick-on-Suir by Poetry Ireland for Poetry Town 2021.

Yanita Georgieva is a Bulgarian poet and journalist based in London. She is a recipient of the 2022 Out-Spoken Prize for Poetry and a member of the Southbank Centre New Poets Collective. You can find her work in bath magg, Poetry Wales, Butcher's Dog, and elsewhere.

James Harris isn't a photographer; he's a walker who takes photos, at stupid o'clock in the morning, on the streets, pathways, parks and beaches of his native Kent, UK. When he's not capturing beauty, he's waging battles against computers which he will never win, but at least he gets paid for it.

Karla Hirsch (she/her) is a German-Romanian writer, editor, and educator. She studied English and French literature in Augsburg and Edinburgh. Her work has been published in *Spry Literary Journal*, *From the Depths*, *Tint Journal* and *433 Magazine*.

Aileen Hunt is a Dublin writer with a particular interest in flash and hybrid forms. Her work has appeared in several online and print journals including The Ogham Stone, Craft, Sweet, Hippocampus, Flashback Fiction and Entropy. You can find her at aileen-hunt.com.

E.E. King is an award-winning painter, writer, and naturalist. She'll do anything that won't pay the bills. She's been published widely, shown paintings at LACMA, painted murals in LA and Spain and is currently painting a mural in a science center. Check out paintings, writing, and books at: www.elizabetheveking.com and amazon.com/author/eeking

Joshua Jones Lofflin's writing has appeared in The Best Microfictions 2020, The Best Small Fictions 2019, The Cincinnati Review, CRAFT, Fractured Lit, Moon City Review, SmokeLong Quarterly, and elsewhere. He lives in Maryland. Find him on Twitter @ jjlofflin or visit his website: jjlofflin.com.

Everly Lovefield is a writer and translator who lives in a town between Houston and Galveston, TX. She holds a BA in French and Japanese from the University of Texas at Austin and an MA in Translation from Kent State University. You can find her on Twitter @everlylovefield.

Simon Maddrell is a queer Manx man, thriving with HIV. He's published in fifteen anthologies and publications including AMBIT, Butcher's Dog, The Moth, The Rialto, Poetry Wales, Stand and Under the Radar. In 2020, Simon's debut poetry collection, Throatbone, was published (UnCollected Press) and pamphlet Queerfella jointly-won The Rialto Open Pamphlet Competition.

Malinda Meadows (she/her) is a Cork-based freelance writer currently working on a collection of poems focusing on grief in the lowercase form: missed birthdays, talking to ghosts, forgotten recipes, the scent of pine cones, and other small, quiet moments.

Ewan Monaghan is a Scottish writer resident in London. He is currently writing a pamphlet about his grandparents. Previous work has been published in The Moth and as part of the AUB International Poetry Prize.

Gráinne Ní Nualláin is a writer, poet, PhD student at UCD, endometriosis/adenomyosis warrior, furious feminist, and cat mom. Find her @grainnenn (Instagram).

Mary O'Donnell's poetry and fiction has been published in Ireland and internationally since1990. Her eighth poetry collection Massacre of the Birds (Salmon) appeared in 2020 and her latest novel is complete. Her work is translated to Portuguese, Spanish and Hungarian. She is a member of Ireland's affiliation of artists, Aosdána. Currently Writer in Residence at the Irish College Leuven during autumn 2022.

Shane O'Driscoll is a visual artist and designer. He studied Visual Communications and is a member of Cork Printmakers and Backwater Artists Group. He has exhibited his work internationally and throughout Ireland. Shane has work in the permanent collection of The National Gallery of Ireland, Trinity College Dublin, UCC, UCD and has also displayed work in The Irish Print Museum. He also has a number of works in the O.P.W. collection. Shane is also a director of Ardú Street Art Project, which creates large scale murals in Cork city.

Katie Oliver is a writer based in Kerry, whose work has been nominated for Best Small Fictions, Best Microfiction and the Pushcart Prize. Her first short story collection, 'I Wanted To Be Close To You', publishes December 2022 with Fly on the Wall Press. She can be found on Twitter @katie_rose_o

Sodïq Oyèkànmí is a Pushcart-nominated poet, a librarian, and a thespian from Ìbàdàn. His works have been published/are forthcoming in North Dakota Quarterly, Poetry Wales, Strange Horizons, VAINE Magazine, trampset, Struggle Magazine, The Orchards Poetry Journal and elsewhere. He was shortlisted for the Lagos — London Poetry Competition. He tweets @sodiqoyekan

Thea Petrou is a translator and writer from London. Her writing on sonnets, tridents and joséphines appears in academic journals and volumes. She recently translated Michèle Métail's 'Letterto S' for the Oxford Anthology of Translation. When not translating, reading, or writing, she can usually be found somewhere in the garden.

Serena Piccoli is an Italian poet, playwright and photographer. She is interested in contemporary social issues. Her latest book of poems is gul\gasp published by Moria Poetry (USA). To see photos and read poems, please visit www.serenapiccoli.com or Twitter: @piccoli_serena

Rory Say is an Irish-Canadian writer of short fiction from Victoria, BC. His stories have appeared in an array of print journals, e-zines and chapbooks, as well as on podcasts. He is currently at work on a full-length collection. Learn more by visiting his website: rorysay.com

Zoey Sibanda Experiencing Michael Angelo's painting 'The Raising of Lazarus' was a catalytic moment for Zoey Sibanda. Could an environment or experience like this be recreated in different mediums to provoke a feeling that motivates audiences to live sustainably? As a multidisciplinary artist, Zoey uses STEM, neuroplasticity and theology-based research to take her audience on a journey exploring this wondrous concept.

Mark Thomas is a retired English and Philosophy teacher, and ex-member of Canada's national rowing team.

We'd like to thank everyone listed below and those who donated anonymously — we couldn't have done it without you.

Trish Bennett
Leopold Bian
Helen Broderick
Roisin Brophy
Ned Brophy
Stephen Buckley
Edmond Burke
Mary Butler
Laura Cassidy
Ailish Cleary-Vertullo
Stephanie Coleman
Eoin Condon
Robyn Coughlan
Maria Coughlan
Luke Cremen
José Croft
Conor Daly
Eilin de Paor
Marie-Annick Desplanques
Orla Doherty
Michelle Donovan
Timothy Dwyer
Kate Ennals
Fiona Ennis
Robyn Foley Buckley
Sian Francis
Eithne Gallagher
Valentina Gindri
Sharon Griffin
Lorraine Haigney
Caitriona Hanley
Siobhan Hanley
James Harris
Colman Hayes
Beth Hewitt
Edward Holloway
Michael Holloway
Barbara Holloway
Jeremy Holme
Jenny Holme
Noel Howley
Ali Isaac
Margaret Kelleher

Tracey Kennedy
Stephanie Larkin
Mary Lyne
Ellen McCarthy
Dominic McDowall
Tony McGettigan
Maeve McGovern
Maria McHale
Ruaidhri McMahon
Malinda Meadows
Zelie Moran
Jenny Mulcahy
Jo Nestor
Catherine Neville
Ailbhe Ni Ghearbhuigh
Kathleen O'Driscoll
David O'Keeffe
Rob O'Halloran
Maura O'Leary
Ruth O'Leary
Keith Payne
Garry Roberts
David Robson
Gwen Roche
Ronan Rooney
Colman Rushe
Charlotte Saunders
Fiona Scannell
Thierry Schreiber
Michelle Sheahan
Anne Tannam
Emma Timmins
Maria Tracey
Diarmaid Twomey
Allegra Van Trojen
Deborah Vogler
Laura Webb
Elizabeth Whittaker

105